PHOENIX

B*

DOLAN, J.

THIS IS A BORZOI BOOK
PUBLISHED BY ALFRED A. KNOPF

Copyright © 2000 by J.D. Dolan

All rights reserved under International and
Pan-American Copyright Conventions.
Published in the United States by Alfred A. Knopf, a division of
Random House, Inc., New York, and simultaneously in Canada by
Random House of Canada Limited, Toronto.
Distributed by Random House, Inc., New York.

www.randomhouse.com

Knopf, Borzoi Books, and the colophon are registered trademarks of
Random House, Inc.

Library of Congress Cataloging-in-Publication Data
Dolan, J.D.
Phoenix : a brother's life / J.D. Dolan. — 1st ed.
p.   cm.
ISBN 0-375-40342-6 (alk. paper)
1. Dolan, J.D.   2. Dolan, John.   3. Brothers—California
Biography.   4. California Biography.   I. Title
CT275.D834A3   2000
979.4'053'099—dc21
[B]   99-33608
CIP

Manufactured in the United States of America
First Edition

7/2000

PHOENIX

A *Brother's* Life

J.D. DOLAN

ALFRED A. KNOPF   *New York*   2000

For their generous help and guidance, I would like to thank Tobias Wolff, Amanda Urban, and Gary Fisketjon.

I would also like to thank Marjory Bassett, Bruce Bauman, Joanne Camacho, Stuart Dybek, Randy Ezratty, Steve Fellner, Jimmy Garcia, Rob Grover, Robin Hemley, Dave Humphrey, Arnie Johnston, Tara Kelly, Al Laven, Fred Leebron, Denice Shannon, Martha Sherrill, Betsy Sussler, Art Winslow, and Tom Wise.

I am grateful to the Virginia Center for the Creative Arts, and to the corporation of Yaddo, for granting me crucial residencies. And for providing me with timely support, I am grateful to the Graduate School of Syracuse University, the Constance Saltonstall Foundation for the Arts, the Irving S. Gilmore Foundation, the Arts Council of Greater Kalamazoo, and Western Michigan University.

Finally, I would like to thank my mother, Arlie B. Dolan, who died while I was finishing the final draft of this book. Her spirit informs every page.

For John

PHOENIX

When I was a little kid, I knew that my brother was lucky. He could stay up late. He could shave. He had a Remington .22 rifle. He was the Master Councilor of the local DeMolay Chapter. He could lay his hands on a dead car engine in the morning and have it purring like a tomcat by midafternoon. When he walked out of our house, he could reach up and touch the top of the doorway, a high, faint smudge offering constant proof. He was lucky in everything—even his looks. He wore button-down shirts and alpaca sweaters, pegged slacks and suede desert boots. He had dark hair and a shy smile—my sisters' friends said in whispered, conspiratorial giggles that he looked like Ricky Nelson—and he smelled of Old Spice, or sometimes motor oil, or sometimes both. But most of all, my brother was lucky because he could go wherever he wanted, and he could go there in his car, a forest green 1950 Chevy two-door with Moon hubcaps and tuck-and-roll upholstery. John was eleven years older, and to me the keys to his car seemed the keys to the world.

Once, a radio station in Los Angeles ran a contest, and whenever you heard a cascade of falling coins, you were supposed to call in. If you were the right caller, you got to guess how much money was in the kitty, and if you guessed right, to the penny, you won it. The caller would guess, and the disc jockey would say, "Puh-*leeze* repeat that!" After the caller repeated the amount, a buzzer would go off, and the disc jockey would say, "I'm *sorry*, that's too . . . *low.*" Or too high. The idea was to listen often and zero in on the amount.

John listened, but not often. At the start of the contest, he guessed a number, wrote it on a piece of paper, and tossed it on the dresser in the bedroom we shared. On that dresser he also kept his wallet, his car keys, his Marlboros, his Old Spice aftershave, his spare change (which he often gave me), a few .22 cartridges, and a black Swank jewelry box where he kept his tie tacks, cuff links, DeMolay pin, and a ruby ring that our grandmother had given him.

After he died, I ended up with some of John's things: a stack of his clothes, a few of his automotive tools, a camera he'd bought in Okinawa, and the jewelry box. Its contents hadn't changed much in twenty-some years. The tie tacks and cuff links were tarnished. The ruby ring was gone (he'd found out it was just red glass). There were some lapel pins from the desert races he'd finished, his Rifle Expert medal, an old key with a Chevrolet logo. Under a tray in the jewelry box I discovered a photograph of our oldest sister, Joanne, at her wedding; grade-school photographs of Janice and June, who were the third and fourth oldest, respectively; also a photograph of me, the youngest, when I was little, and one of our parents from a time before I knew them, when they were still, from the looks of it, in love.

Another photograph, a small one of my brother and my father, still filled me with a kind of grinning wonder. In this one photograph, my brother's about two and my father's in his early thirties. My father is standing in front of my grandmother's house with one arm stretched out high, and my brother is standing in the palm of his hand. I remember looking at that photograph when I was little and saying, "And *who's* that little boy? And *who's* that man?" When they told me, I accepted it the same way I did when Dad would pull quarters out of my ear or when John somehow knew just when a red light was going to turn green. I knew it was some kind of trick of the adult world, and I played along.

John called the radio station a few times but couldn't get through. He didn't have a lot of time to listen to contests; he was working overtime as a supermarket clerk and saving his money for—though it didn't seem possible—an even *better* car.

I listened to the radio station every day after school and kept track of the contest. With each call, with each wrong guess, it seemed John was that much closer to winning.

One day, as I rode with my mother to the supermarket in our Oldsmobile, I switched on the radio. I sang along to Ricky Nelson's "Travelin' Man," then quieted down when I heard the familiar cascade of falling coins.

The contest! This was it! A woman caller made a guess, and the disc jockey said, "Puh-*leeze* repeat that!" Something about that number was familiar, and as she repeated it, I screamed, "That's *John's* number!" My mother—nervous in her menopausal years—nearly ran the Olds into a parked car. She started yelling at me, but all I could hear just then were the sounds of bells and whistles, and an even greater rush of falling coins.

The radio station played that winning call over and over the next few days. That winning number, John's number, was, I thought, fixed in my memory. But I've forgotten it, just as I'm beginning to forget John's voice. Not surprisingly. He didn't talk much to begin with, and it's been eleven years since his death, and for the last five years of his life he wouldn't talk to me, then he died.

John took the news of the contest, as he did most news, with a shrug. He seemed to have, even in those days, a belief that life was somehow rigged, that even with the right numbers he was destined to lose.

That isn't the way I saw it. But for a phone call he'd won that radio contest. He could work automotive miracles. He could reach impossible heights. He looked like Ricky Nelson. He had the keys to the world and the gas money to get there. My brother was lucky. And I knew that soon, very soon, his number would come up.

His number came up a few days before Christmas in 1965. His draft number. John was ordered to report on January 4, 1966, for induction into the United States Army.

I was thrilled! My brother loved to watch the movie *Sergeant York* and the TV show *Combat,* and therefore I loved to watch them too. I knew my brother would be shrewd like Gary Cooper and tough like Vic Morrow. And when he came home, I knew my brother and I would be just like the TV show *Route 66*—two guys driving around the country in a Corvette convertible in search of excitement. I knew this because John had sold his forest green 1950 Chevy two-door and, with all of his savings, bought an immaculate red 1958 Corvette convertible. The countless TV mythologies of my childhood—shy teen idols, patriotic soldiers, free spirits in fast cars—had become one, it seemed, and achieved flesh and blood in my brother.

The afternoon before Christmas, John waxed his car out on the driveway, covering it with whorls of pale greenish wax until the car looked like a ghost of itself. John didn't like to do his waxing in bright sunlight—partial shade was always better, he said—but wanted to give the car one last coat before he was drafted; besides, this was only winter sunlight, bright and weak, the kind that looks warm but isn't. As he slowly rubbed away the dried wax with the folded cheesecloth, the red Corvette began to shine like a Christmas tree ornament.

Our ash tree in the front yard had been steadily losing its leaves for the last week, and the dry brown leaves were falling thick as snow on our dry brown lawn—which made for great sliding. I hid behind the variegated ivy that framed the front porch, a good toy soldier in one hand, an evil toy soldier in the other: waiting until just the right time. Then I made a run for the spread of leaves and shrieked like a dive-bomber, and then became the bomb and hit the leaves sliding, and the leaves became smoke—there were screaming and machine-gun fire!—and gradually, you could see the good soldier rising heroically from the rubble. With my sneakers I stubbed the leaves back into place, then skipped across the lawn to the front porch and hid behind the ivy again, good in one hand, evil in the other, and waited.

When our father was due home from work, I sat on the fire hydrant at the corner until I saw his old yellow-and-white De Soto in the distance. Then I crossed the street, and he pulled up and stopped—our daily routine—as I climbed onto the big chrome bumper and held tight to the hood ornament, a bust of the helmeted De Soto himself. With me clinging to the warm hood, my father drove slowly past our yellow tract house, then sped up slightly as he made the U-turn and pulled up in front, swirling leaves, braking evenly until the last few feet, where he stopped the car with a little jolt, and I let go of the hood ornament and, for a moment, could fly.

John watched, grinning, from the driveway.

As my father walked toward the house, I trotted alongside, carrying his old beat-up briefcase and wearing his smart Greyhound cap, which fit my head like a tent.

John nodded hello and wiped the sweat from his forehead with the back of his hand. He seemed to be contemplating his wax job.

Dad nodded hello back, then veered over to the driveway beside John. They didn't look at each other, only at the car, and probably at their elongated reflections in the mirrored finish.

"Looks good," Dad said.

This was a tense moment. It had been months since the two of them had said anything more to each other than a grumbled "hello," and usually they didn't even say that much. I didn't understand what all of this was about, just that it had started when Joanne stayed out past her curfew and was ordered by our father to move out. John had been mad about it, and my mother had been nervous, and Janice and June had begun a turf war over the new space this opened up in the big bedroom that until then the three girls had shared pretty happily.

I set the briefcase on the lawn, took off the Greyhound cap.

John wiped a speck of wax from the door handle. "Well," he said, "it'll help protect it."

Dad looked at John and said, "You're not going to leave it out here, are you?" as if his greatest worry about his oldest son getting drafted was that his son's car would be prey to the elements.

John shrugged at this hopeless situation and said, "And the battery will probably go dead," as if his greatest worry about getting drafted was whether his car would start when he got back.

At the time, those were probably my greatest worries, too.

My father shook his head. "No. No. Keep it in the garage. I can start it up once a week. I'll keep an eye on it."

John didn't say anything, but I could tell, from the way his shoulders dropped a little, that he was relieved.

My father picked up the briefcase, took the Greyhound cap from my hands, and said, walking away, "I'll tune it up before you get back."

With John and Dad on seemingly good terms again, the world seemed a wonderful place, a lucky place to be alive for. I went back to playing in the dead leaves and, once exhausted, lay there on my back and stared up at the immense blue sky and the faint high clouds, and as the clouds moved it felt as if the earth was turning. I could see the snowy peak of Mount Baldy, which was usually hidden in smog but now seemed to stand out in high relief on top of the Cannons' house across the street. John kept working on the Corvette, vacuuming the interior, wiping down the dash, polishing the gauges. He'd turned on the radio, and Elvis sang of blue Christmases and Bing sang of white ones. It was getting dark, and one by one our neighbors' Christmas lights came on, then ours did, and in Hollywood, probably at some movie premiere, searchlights fanned bars of light across our sky. I heard something overhead—it sounded as if the sky was humming—and finally I saw it, just another ordinary miracle: the huge silver blimp cruising the San Gabriel Valley in preparation for next week's Rose Parade, its side spelling out the truth in giant spotlighted letters: GOODYEAR.

Our Christmas tree was done up with bright ornaments and flashing lights, and our house smelled of pine needles and pumpkin pies and sugar cookies, and the cotton batting under the tree was heaped with gifts wrapped in paper patterned with Santas and snowflakes and HO!

HO! HO! If I'd thought at all about John getting drafted, it was as part of the Christmas pageant. What I'd thought about mostly the last week, the last month, was an elaborate toy-gun set with suction-cup bullets and a painted tin bull's-eye with twirling ducks on top. For this I'd been lobbying my mother relentlessly.

I got up early—very early—on Christmas morning and slid quietly from the top bunk. I didn't want to wake John sneaking out of our bedroom.

The living room was dark except for the tree's flashing lights, but that was all the light I'd need to snoop through the gifts. I knew I'd probably get what I wanted, but then again, I knew what to want. And I knew that the card would be signed FROM MOM & DAD, and that another gift, a package of underwear from J. C. Penney, would have a card signed FROM SANTA. Both cards would be written in my mother's frantic, loopy cursive. My gifts to my parents displayed a similar flair. Every Christmas, I got my father a carton of Chesterfield Kings and my mother some sort of toiletry that stank of lavender or lilac.

With Joanne and John it was different.

John was eleven when I was born, and Mom liked to tell the story of how he'd always wanted a little brother. He already had an older sister, Joanne, and two younger sisters, Janice and June. Still, when I was born, he apparently wasn't happy about it. "What's wrong?" my mother asked him. "I thought you *wanted* a little brother."

"I wanted one *my* size," he said.

My mom would always laugh after she told that story, then say, "I should send that one to *Reader's Digest*."

Joanne, at twelve, was happy to have a little brother. She'd grown tired of raising her dolls, so she set them aside and raised me instead. When I was a little older, and at least closer to his size, John also helped with that effort. My parents, I'm sure, appreciated it. My mother was forty-two when I was born, my father forty-three, and during most of my childhood they were busy and distracted—plus they'd already gone a good way toward raising four other kids, and were no doubt somewhat tired. My father had joined the Masonic Lodge and was working his way up through the Line, as it was called; he was already a Junior Deacon, and eventually would become Master of the Ramona Lodge. My mother had joined the Eastern Star, which meant mostly that she was a Masonic wife, helping out with the many dinners and pancake breakfasts, and especially the installations—big affairs with women in formals and men in tuxedos. These were the years that my mother came to think of as her change of life, which to her was synonymous with nervousness, confusion, and sadness. She'd sometimes smile and say to me, without a bit of intended irony, "And you were my change-of-life baby."

But my parents' distractions didn't bother me much, if at all; I probably noticed my parents about as much as they noticed me. I liked hanging out at the Masonic Lodge, which was also called the Job's Daughter Bethel and the DeMolay Chapter and the Eastern Star Chapter, different names for the same place—the Lodge is what everybody called it. I could make elegant noise on the upright piano in the big empty dining room, or roll the bright-colored balls around the green baize of the pool table, or sit little and innocent in the women's powder room with Joanne, the Job's Daughters' Honored Queen (honest to god, that was the title), and sneak looks as all the Jobies prepared themselves for the Installation. I watched them roll white stockings up into the dark regions of their legs, watched them snap bras against their pale backs, watched them hold their necks just so and lean into the vanity mirror and apply frosted pink lipstick until their lips shined like fresh candy, watched them fluff their poofed-out formals and dab perfume behind their ears until they looked and smelled like giant flowers.

"Hey, what's *he* doing in here?" some Joby said at some point in my growth, and I was scooted out of the women's powder room forever. I sulked for a while downstairs in the pool room, and then I went down to the parking lot and hung out with my big brother, the DeMolays' Master Councilor, and stood around with him and all the other DeMolays, who smoked Marlboros and regarded their car engines and mumbled their secret desires about the Jobies I'd already known so intimately.

As I was growing up, Joanne and John weren't exactly like parents to me—they were better. They took me places, and not because they had to but because they liked to. Joanne would take me shopping or to the movies or the beach, and John would take me fishing or target shooting or out on long drives in the desert. One of the main reasons they took me places, I imagine, is that I absolutely adored them both, and one of the main reasons I adored them is because my parents had vested them with an authority over me that was equal to their own, and because Joanne and John exercised this authority by being kind.

I don't mean to say that Joanne and John were alike—she was friendly and outgoing, whereas he was shy and often cynical—but to me they were alike in all the ways that mattered.

This was evident, especially, at Christmas. Each of them always got me something special, nothing it would've occurred to me to want, and that always seemed to get better the longer I owned it. One year, Joanne gave me my first pocketknife, a two-blade model with shiny black scales. Another year, John gave me a brass compass with a snap-open top. I don't know if these gifts could have meant as much to me if anyone else had given them. I just knew that Joanne and John had a knack for getting me what I wanted before I even knew I did—and that's why I sneaked into the living room that Christmas morning.

I'd spent a lot of time considering what to get the two of them this Christmas, since Joanne had been banished from our house a few months earlier, and John was getting drafted the following week. For Joanne, I'd pestered J. C. Penney's salesladies with questions about the quality of silk scarves and the effectiveness of natural-bristle hairbrushes, but finally settled on a reversible tortoise-shell hand mirror, one side of which made your face look gigantic. For John, I'd studied the Swank wallets and belts in Men's Accessories (while Santa was off buying, among other things, my underwear). I'd been noodling over every item for a good half hour when a crusty old salesman came over and said, "Interested in that alligator belt, young man?" I looked at him coldly and said, "It's alligator *cowhide*." This was a difficult Christmas, given that I wanted to get John something he could take with him to Vietnam, and J. C. Penney didn't seem to offer much in the way of jungle gear. But I finally decided on the Deluxe Old Spice Gift Set, which came with its own leather shaving kit and was—its selling point—waterproof.

On Christmas morning, my presents to them were there on the cotton batting, along with my presents to Janice and June, Mom and Dad, and all of their presents to me. I inspected every one, careful not to let one of the boughs snag on my flannel pajamas and jar loose one of the frail ornaments: mirrored glass balls that seemed designed to fall off, roll around, and break.

Everything was just where it should be. Santa had gotten me some underwear. June had gotten me a Superman lunch bucket—a really neat present. Janice had asked me a few days earlier if I wanted a pencil box, and I'd told her I didn't use a pencil box, didn't want a pencil box, and wouldn't be caught dead with a pencil box. Janice had gotten me a pencil box. Joanne had gotten me something wrapped so well I couldn't tell what was inside. (It turned out to be a real camera—with flashbulbs!) Then I saw a big present leaning against the wall and realized, with a kind of dull thrill, that my Christmas-gift lobbying of my mother had worked: I knew from its size and shape that my elaborate toy-gun set was inside, and I knew, even without opening the box, that the gun set would never be as shiny and bright as it had been in Penney's toy section; the rifle would be made of plastic, the twirling ducks wouldn't twirl, the target would eventually dent.

But I couldn't find whatever it was that John had gotten me, and I was beginning to wonder if he'd gotten me anything at all.

It wasn't quite dark outside anymore. Our windows had lightened to the color of tin, and the rest of the living room began to take shape: the big buffet over by the door, Dad's La-Z-Boy, the sofa, the swivel-base TV, and something propped up in the corner that hadn't been there before, something tall and thin and dark and—I could just now make out—with a red bow tied around it.

I hadn't expected to see anything in the corner, and therefore didn't quite believe it. I thought I must be seeing things wrong, or that maybe there wasn't enough light yet, or that maybe I was *dreaming* I was awake, because John always kept his .22 rifle in one corner of our bedroom, but now it was in the corner by the Christmas tree. I took a few steps toward it. From the red bow tied around the walnut stock there hung a small card.

FOR J.D.

LOVE, JOHN

For a few minutes I just stood there—I didn't even touch it. I'd been hoping for a crappy toy gun and twirling duck targets. I hadn't even bothered hoping for a BB gun. But this—this was a *real* gun, a rifle, a Remington; it had been my father's, then my brother's, and now it was mine. I picked up the rifle, slung its leather strap across my shoulder. The walnut stock was cool and smooth, and the rifle felt even heavier than I remembered—the weight of authority, responsibility. The weight of the whole grown-up world. I stood tall, as if ready to have a war medal pinned on my chest.

Then I ran back into the bedroom with the rifle and scream-whispered, "Hey, John!"

John, about to be drafted into the Army and shipped off to Vietnam, must have also thought he was dreaming, seeing his little brother suddenly standing there in the early morning light beside his bed, holding a rifle in a soldier's pose. He sat up fast and there was a sound like a bat on a softball as his head hit the boards on the underside of the top bunk. The covers on the top mattress lifted slightly, then settled.

"Thanks for the rifle," I said, wincing.

John nodded and, with his hand pressed against his forehead, said, "Merry Christmas."

When my mother saw that John had given me the .22, she had, as John liked to describe it, "a conniption fit."

"You could *kill* somebody with that thing!" she said.

I think she meant to frighten me, but instead I said, *"Really?"*

"It's okay," John said, "we're going target shooting later."

If anyone else had given me a .22 rifle, my mother probably would've shot him with it. But to John she only shook her head nervously and said, "Oh, well, be careful."

That afternoon, as we carried our rifles outside, I felt like we were soldiers going off to war. We walked like soldiers, we were serious like soldiers, we even smelled like soldiers, I figured, because I'd splashed on some of John's Old Spice aftershave. When we got in the Corvette, John sniffed twice, looked over at me, and turned the key in the ignition. The Corvette's engine—that low rumble—sounded like a bomber squadron at takeoff.

On the way out of town, we stopped and picked up one of John's best friends, Mickey Otten. They'd been in the DeMolays for the last five years, along with their other best friend, Glen Burbank. Neither Mickey nor Glen was going to be drafted; Mickey had flat feet, and Glen was already half deaf. None of John's friends would get to fight in Vietnam, and I felt sorry for them; it seemed as if the luckiest thing about them was that they knew my brother.

With the three of us crammed into the Corvette, we headed out Route 66 toward the desert. It was raining lightly, but a little rain wasn't going to stop soldiers like us—and by "us" I meant John and me.

I woke up as we were coming down the Cajon Pass, on the back side of the San Gabriel Mountains and the edge of the Mojave. John turned onto a dirt road and drove for a few miles, then parked on a rise overlooking a floodplain cut by hundreds of tiny streams—the runoff from the foothills. We set out across it single file with our rifles and hiked until we found a good slope littered with rusted tin cans and—don't ask me how—a fender from an old Ford pickup.

I learned very quickly that it would be some time before anybody had to worry about losing his life to my marksmanship. My arms were soon tired from lifting the rifle, so I tended to aim low, and about the only thing I could hit with any frequency was the fender, and that only at close range. I fired about a million rounds into the sand and then dug out the two slugs I could find, and saved them for good luck.

John had bought himself a Ruger semiautomatic in a padded vinyl case, and he shot that rifle like an expert. He aimed carefully at each tin can, pulled the trigger slowly: the tin can jumped. "You're not going to have any trouble over there!" Mickey said. John grinned, took aim, shot again, and Mickey said, "They better cover their asses!" This went on for a long time, John shooting and Mickey cheering. But Mickey ran out of cheers before my brother ran out of ammo. That's when Mickey said, "You know . . . maybe you should try shooting at a *moving* target."

For a long time, neither of them said anything. Mickey stared at the ground in front of his feet. John fiddled with the rifle's sight, then put the rifle back in its case. The rain was coming down heavier now, and the sky was getting dark.

I was still excited from what I called our "hunting trip," and on the day before his induction, as John picked up his car keys and his Marlboros from the dresser, I jumped down from the top bunk and followed him into the living room. "Where you going?" I said. I was a grown-up, a soldier, one of the guys, and wanted to go along.

"For a drive."

"Can I go?"

John thought for a moment, then said, very kindly, "Not this time, Jay."

I nodded as if this made complete sense, although I'm sure the twitching corners of my mouth betrayed the way I really felt. I didn't feel like a grown-up or a soldier, because while I'd understood that John was leaving the next day, it wasn't until this moment that I realized he might not come back. I looked away, toward the Christmas tree. It was brittle and didn't smell much of Christmas anymore; its needles were falling off, and it looked naked without the presents, and the cotton batting did not remotely look like snow.

As he walked out of the house, John didn't touch the top of the doorway—he just walked out.

I heard the Corvette's engine growl to life and then fade away, and I ran in and climbed up on the bunk bed and gulped air, the side of my face pressed into my soon-wet pillow. John was going off to the Army, to Vietnam, and he might never come home, and the weight of the grown-up world had me pinned to my mattress.

After a few minutes I heard a rumbling—that engine!—and looked out the window and saw the Corvette come to a smart stop on our driveway, heard the familiar ratcheted sound of my brother setting the parking brake. I was running toward the door when John walked back into the house.

John looked at me and smiled. "C'mon, buddy," he said, and this time he touched the top of the doorway as he walked out.

I didn't ask where we were going. It didn't matter. We just headed out Route 66, out into the desert, and neither of us said anything because we didn't need to. We didn't have to get anywhere; we just drove for the pure pleasure of driving, of being out on the road, together.

When we got back home, John didn't park on the driveway; he pulled all the way into the garage, wiped down the Corvette with a chamois, buffed it with a sheepskin mitt, and covered it with a canvas tarp.

The evening news on TV always ended with the day's body count in Vietnam. But my brother was lucky. He was not drafted into the United States Army. Instead, he was drafted into the United States Marine Corps; for the first time since World War II, the Marines had resorted to a draft. They had an urgent need at the front lines for a few good men, and my brother, I thought proudly, was going to be one of them—a leatherneck! A Marine! A hero!

My brother didn't come home a war hero. He just came home two inches taller and a little more cynical. He even told me that he'd held his breath when he was asked to breathe during his induction physical, but they'd certified him fit anyway.

Even in the Corps, my brother was lucky. After his basic training at Camp Pendleton, he received orders for a thirteen-month tour of duty in Vietnam. He'd learned how to throw a hand grenade, launch a mortar, shoot an M-14. He'd learned to speak rudimentary Vietnamese. He could pump out a hundred push-ups and run ten miles with a full pack. On the flight to Vietnam, his plane stopped for fuel in Naha, Okinawa, where the Marine Corps needed two men—*now*. Two were chosen at random and ordered off the flight. John was one of them. He spent the next thirteen months working in a warehouse at Camp Kinser, in Urasoe City, Okinawa, where he drove a five-ton truck and processed the belongings of the dead. (Some of the presents he sent us that next Christmas were packed with old Marine Corps fatigues, some of which, I noticed, had bullet holes in them.) On his days off, he saw the countryside, became interested in photography, and now and then, for drinking money between paychecks, pawned his ruby ring for two bucks. Of the 118 men in his company who went on to combat in Vietnam, only 13 came home alive. And though he didn't return a war hero, John did take me for drives in his red Corvette—often out in the desert on Route 66. If I learned *how* to drive from watching my father, a Greyhound bus driver, I *wanted* to drive from watching my brother in his infinite good luck: from seeing his profile set against the Mojave Desert, and from feeling myself pressed back against the passenger seat as he shifted gears and floored the Corvette and all the world around us became a blur.

I heard an engine like that one night, about twenty years later, in Phoenix, where John lay in a hospital bed with third-degree thermal burns—steam burns—over 90 percent of his body, with chances of survival about equal to the percentage of skin he had left. His odds were not impossible, though his situation was. If he died, it would be tragic. If he lived, it would be worse.

My mother and my three sisters and I had left the burn unit late in the evening and eaten another sullen dinner together before going back to the hotel. I was just falling asleep when I heard it—a car with a big engine, probably with a four-barrel carb and dual exhausts, the kind of engine that you feel as much as hear. And as that big-engined car rumbled to a stop and its parking brake ripped the night in two, I sat up wide awake in the dark and wondered, just for a moment, if some sort of rescue was at hand.

The phone call came to me in Paris. I was staying on the Île St.-Louis, in a beautiful apartment on loan from a rich friend in New York City. It was early afternoon, sunny and quiet, an easy warmth angling through the old window glass onto the worn oak floors. I'd just come in from lunch and a long walk, my usual routine. I'd been there about two weeks, while waiting out the publication of my first story—an event that had me so overloaded with anticipation that I'd borrowed some money, taken a few weeks off from my bartending job on the Upper East Side, and flown to Paris in an effort, really, to get away from myself.

I had nobody to talk to, not that I could've talked to anybody anyway—my French was for *merde*. So I walked a lot, sat in cafés, wrote in my journal, came back, and settled into the soft leather sofa and the soft light in a lovely, solitary apartment. Until that afternoon when the telephone rang.

I wasn't expecting any calls. I hadn't even left any-body my number. My whereabouts were no great secret, but if somebody needed to reach me, he'd have to have a good reason or bad news to track me down.

My brother-in-law Ernie had both. I could hear it in the false cheer of his hey-how-you-doin' voice, and my first thought, or at least my first clenched impulse, was that this was the call telling me my mother was dead. I'd grown up with parents who were nearly as old as most of my friends' grandparents, and when I was quite young I got the notion that my mother and father were going to drop dead at any minute, most likely while I was asleep. Some nights, I'd go and stand sleepy-eyed in my Bugs Bunny pajamas at the doorway of their bedroom, strain-ing to see by the patches of blue streetlight coming from the cracks in their curtains, watching for the rise and fall of their chests until I was sure they were still breathing, still alive, before shuffling back to my bed. People had often mistaken my oldest sister, Joanne, for my mother as she wheeled me in a shopping cart through the Alpha Beta; later, out at the desert races, a few people had even mistaken my brother, John, for my father. These were mistakes I sometimes made myself.

My father had already died, less than a year earlier, at seventy, and as I held the telephone and listened to my brother-in-law's voice ("Hey, Jay, how you doin'?"), I knew soon enough that this wasn't about my mother. To be hearing and speaking English felt as strange as hearing the particular words he used to describe what had happened to my brother and fifteen others. Some of what had happened, Ernie couldn't even put into words. Some of what he did put into words, I

25

couldn't understand. "It doesn't," he said, and paused, "look good."

My brother's life was contained in that pause.

It was clear that my brother might die, but all I could think of just then was that he might also live—and if he did live, the son of a bitch, would he finally see fit to speak to me?

My mother, Ernie went on to say, was fine. She and my sisters had already flown from Los Angeles to the burn unit in Phoenix.

That Ernie had called was strange—John hadn't talked to him in years, either. "Should I fly home?" I managed to make myself say, and Ernie, in one of his finer moments, said without hesitation, "Yes."

Outside, Paris was, remarkably enough, still Paris. I put on my sunglasses and stepped into a mid-June postcard: blue sky with wisps of high clouds, bright, warm sunshine, cool shade from the old stone buildings. I walked the half block up Rue Poulletier to the Seine, where I turned and headed down Quai d'Anjou to the southeastern tip of the Île St.-Louis, trying to sort out what Ernie had told me.

I stopped on the Pont de Sully and looked out over the little park at the tip of the island. A tourist boat motored by, churning a wake that sparkled in the sunlight like broken glass. A soft wind, swaying the big leafy poplars along the banks, held the faint scent of diesel. Here at the point where the Seine parts, with the waters flowing to the Left Bank on one side of me and the Right Bank on the other, it seemed as if the island itself was a boat moving forward at good speed, and I was on it.

I leaned heavily on the bridge's warm cement rail. I couldn't imagine what a body would look like with its skin burned away. What would hold the bones inside? What would contain the blood? I walked slowly through the touristy middle of the Île St.-Louis, then crossed the bridge to the Île de la Cité, where the spires of Notre Dame, just up ahead, pierced the sky. All around me people walked idly or rested on benches in the shade. They ate elegant little ice cream cones from Berthillon and smoked rich-smelling cigarettes. They squinted up at the cathedral, their hands raised to shield their eyes from the sun, their mouths open in silent awe. They posed awkwardly for snapshots of themselves with God looming in the background.

I kept thinking about what Ernie had told me, kept trying to put it into perspective. I didn't know if third-degree burns were the worst, and this lack of knowledge felt like a moral failure. I quickened my pace a little at the thought that maybe there were fourth-degree burns—or that maybe first-degree burns were the worst. I'd forgotten to ask Ernie about that. There seemed to be a lot of questions I'd forgotten, and the flying buttresses and high stone walls of Notre Dame offered no answers, or at least not the ones I wanted.

Ernie had said, "It doesn't . . . look good." He'd meant that it didn't look like John was going to live, but neither did it look good otherwise.

I kept walking, I don't remember where or for how long, until I found myself in front of a shopwindow, and looked inside. I was wearing a pair of mirrored Vuarnet sunglasses just like the ones spread out on blue velvet behind the glass. I'd looked in this same window a week earlier, with the thought of buying my brother a good pair of sunglasses, a small peace offering disguised as something practical. I'd heard from my mother that John worked for Edison now, at their power plant out in the Mojave. She said he liked his job. He had a lot of friends. He was even buying a house. And of course, she said, he loved the desert. For the first time in years, it sounded as if he was actually happy, as if he was engaged by a better life. I felt the same about my own life. So I thought that maybe—I didn't want to think about it too much, but just *maybe*—if I could find the right gift . . .

This posed a lot of problems. I'd thought about a Swiss Army knife, something John could use (I imagined him keeping it in his glove compartment), but a gift from Switzerland didn't really make sense; I was, after all, in France. I sniffed at dozens of colognes, after-shaves, shaving soaps. These were from France, but were also, I could hear my brother saying, *phony*, which to him was the same as pretentious. I looked at Cartier cigarette lighters but wasn't sure if he still smoked; besides that, they were phony too. I fingered lacquered fountain pens, silk ties, Egyptian cotton dress shirts—phony, phony, phony. And useless in the desert. There were probably a lot of things in Paris that my brother would have liked, but none of them seemed to be displayed in shopwindows for tourists, at least not for this tourist. It had been years since I'd talked to him. I wasn't sure anymore what my brother would like because I wasn't sure who he was. I was about ready to give up when I saw the sunglasses.

This should've been simple. My Vuarnets looked not unlike the classic Ray-Bans that John had worn for years. And they had mirrored bronze-colored lenses; instead of darkening the world to a smoky gray, they filtered out the harsh glare of sunlight while somehow making everything else brighter and bringing it into high relief. I liked the idea of giving my brother a brighter outlook on the world.

The desert, my brother, sunglasses. Perfect. I was about to go inside and buy him a pair like mine, but then I wondered if he'd *want* a pair like mine. There was a sportier model, with lenses a bit larger and more rounded, that would look perfect on a skier or a lifeguard. I'd almost bought that model for myself. But this gift was for my brother, and in this way it had political implications. If I bought him identical sunglasses, he might think I was hinting that he should be more like me—making my gift, really, just a subtle dig. And if I got him the sportier pair, he might wonder why I chose the classic model for myself. He was no skier, no lifeguard— he might consider these sunglasses a comment on all that he was not. And what if I gave him the gift and he didn't even open it? What if he just sneered at me and nudged the box away? What if he did nothing except walk out of the house?

Well, that's up to John, I thought. I was going to get him some sunglasses—once I decided which ones. But there was no rush, I thought, I'd be in Paris for weeks. I could come back anytime.

And I did. I came back to the same shop a week later and looked at the same sunglasses spread out on the same blue velvet, but everything else had changed. If I'd bought John that gift when I should have—I was sure of this—the accident would never have happened. Somehow, with the momentum of that simple gesture the planets would have aligned themselves differently, the stars—everything would've been different. Ridiculous, I know, but that's how it felt.

I should have bought him the sunglasses the week before, but couldn't bring myself to buy them now. The gesture seemed cheap and wrong, possibly cruel. He might have been blinded in the blast, or be laid up in a hospital bed for the rest of his life. He might fetch up dead. And even if he didn't, even if he survived and needed a pair of sunglasses, he still might not want them in the form of some patronizing gift from me.

I stared at my image in the shopwindow, at my tiny image in my sunglass lenses, at my even tinier image in all the sunglasses on display, and every one of them stared back at me with an expression that said, in a language unburdened by words, *You fucked up.*

On the flight from Paris to Los Angeles (a crowded, bargain-airline flight with delays taking off, with spilled drinks and falling luggage, arguing passengers, sick passengers, and screaming babies), I sat wedged into my seat and stared into my eyelids, thinking about the last time I'd seen my brother.

It was eight or ten months ago—Jesus, nearly a year. Then, as now, I wasn't sure what I was flying home to. Ernie, often our family's bearer of bad news, had called me in New York City to say my father was dying in the hospital and that I should probably catch the next flight to Los Angeles. "I think this is really it," he'd added. Every few years for the last decade, my father had gone into the hospital with something about ready to kill him: a heart attack, a blood clot, more heart attacks, and once, during some routine arthritis treatment, he'd suffered a blood clot *and* a heart attack. Every time, we'd congregated there at the hospital—

except I was working on the road then, and missed about half of my father's near deaths—and every time he'd somehow pulled through, coming home a little more frail and withered, further wracked with arthritis. Every few years he'd suffer a big relapse, go in for a month or two, and we'd all huddle as if to witness the end. The end came five or six times. What Ernie had meant was, this is *really* it.

He met me at the boarding gate, gave me an awkward hug and said, "How you doin'?" Then he said, "I'm sorry, Jay. You almost made it. Your father passed away a few hours ago." It sounded as if these were lines that Ernie had rehearsed.

I said, "How's my mom holding up?"

Ernie smiled and said, "Better than your sisters."

My three nephews were at the airport, too. Ernie and Joanne's two sons, Jeff and Mike, and Janice's son, Eric. Jeff and Eric were the same age, about fourteen, and Mike was a couple of years older. They took my shoulder bag, my carry-on bags, and I could see that they liked showing me they were bigger than the last time I'd seen them, liked having new muscles, liked helping out. Jeff swung one of my bags over his shoulder. I could see a flash of braces in his mouth as he said, "Sorry about Grandpa, Uncle Jay." I wasn't really sorry that my father had died, although there was much in his life I was sorry about. I wasn't really even thinking about my father's death. What I was thinking about just then was my nephews. They were such sweet kids. But kids, transparent as glass. In my earliest memories of my brother—at fourteen or fifteen—he'd seemed to me a gigantic figure, a grown-up, an inscrutable god. To imagine that John had ever been a kid like this—or that he'd ever been a kid at all—was virtually impossible.

John wasn't along the next day, when we went to make my father's funeral arrangements at Rose Hills Memorial Park. I'd been to about a million funerals at Rose Hills when I was a kid—my grandmother's funeral, an uncle's funeral, the funeral of the little kid I knew across the street who'd died in his sleep, countless Masonic funerals for desiccated geezers from my father's lodge. The huge ROSE HILLS sign, done up like the famous HOLLYWOOD sign except in pink neon, had been visible from every vantage point in our neighborhood—from all over the San Gabriel Valley, in fact—and could even be seen from our front yard until the dump on the other side of the freeway grew too high. So it was familiar but creepy to be here at Rose Hills, making our own arrangements for the first time and finally going into the big showroom, where each casket was waxed and spotlighted and displayed like something from the Los Angeles Auto Show, to which my brother had once taken me.

I wished John had been there with us, partly because I thought he might accidentally let his guard down and start talking to me again, and partly because I knew he'd be a calming influence on our mother and our three sisters—particularly the younger two—and that he'd increase, however slightly, the chances our family might actually agree on something, particularly Janice and Mom. They'd waged a bitter, jealous war with each other for years—forever—over the attentions of my father, and this seemed like the perfect site for one last battle.

Joanne, the oldest, led Mom from casket to casket, and they talked quietly, sometimes turning to ask a question of the not-at-all-ghoulish funeral director, who stood patiently at the doorway of the showroom and simply let our guilt perform the sales pitch. The high-end caskets looked like bank vaults made of burnished brass, with spacious interiors tufted in white satin and trimmed with lace that looked as inviting as a comfy daybed on a rainy afternoon. These might as well have been labeled WE LOVE YOU, WE'LL ALWAYS LOVE YOU. The low-end caskets had skimpy handles and a finish that looked like mouse fur. They looked cramped and uncomfortable and might as well have been labeled WE ARE CHEAP AND UNGRATEFUL.

June drifted around the showroom like an unmoored boat.

Janice stared at one of the top-end caskets and twirled a strand of dark brown hair around her finger—a nervous habit that always reminded me of the goofy gesture people make to indicate someone's crazy.

We all went back into the funeral director's little office, where Joanne took the lead and started going through some of the practical matters of the burial ("And the difference between the two caskets is, this one's waterproof?"), weighing the costs and the options. June just sat there in high-idle, smoking a cigarette, and only once interjected a semihostile question ("*Which* casket is waterproof?"), as if we'd been trying to exclude her from the process. After the funeral director answered, she settled back into her brooding.

34

Janice also sat there smoking a cigarette. She and June both smoked Tareytons. I thought of how they used to watch from the front window of our living room when, twenty years earlier, Joanne would pull onto our driveway in her white Thunderbird and emerge like a movie star with a Tareyton scissored between two fingers. Since then, Joanne had quit smoking, but Janice and June were still emulating her in other ways.

Joanne had started working at Southern California Edison a few years earlier, after she'd discovered one of Ernie's affairs and separated from him for a while, and it wasn't long before June started working there too, and then Janice. Not too long ago, they'd also found John a job out in the desert, at one of Edison's power plants. *My family*, I thought. And then I thought, *Inertia.*

"This one will be fine," my mother said with surprising finality. She'd chosen a simple, handsome steel casket painted dark gray. She began going down the list, saying exactly what we did and didn't need.

I looked over at Janice. If there was going to be a battle, this was the time. She didn't like agreeing with our mother on anything—not even tacit agreement, and certainly not anything about our father—but all she did was blink a few times and draw deeply on her cigarette. Several cremation urns were on display in the funeral director's office, and one sat on a low table beside Janice's chair. She looked at the cigarette and then looked around the room. The funeral director was reaching for the ashtray on his desk, but Janice had already spotted the urn, which evidently looked to her like a fancy ashtray, which, I guess, it was. I was about to say something to her but thought better; it seldom did any good to tell Janice anything. She tapped the ashes into the lid of the urn, took one long last drag on the cigarette, then stubbed out the butt with three quick pecks. She looked up and started twirling a strand of hair again. The funeral director deftly slid the ashtray out of sight. He never said a word about it.

At my father's funeral, I sat between Mom and John. This was a Masonic funeral, notable mostly for the Masonic aprons the men wore, and by the phrase "so mote it be" instead of "amen." It was obvious that my father's ancient friends knew the funeral routines well: they knew where to park, and when the whole thing was about to wrap up; they looked comfortable in their shiny funeral suits. I'd been to plenty of funerals growing up; they'd been to a whole lot more.

One Mason got up and told an anecdote about my father that I'd never heard. He recalled a trip to the Grand Lodge in San Francisco. "I was walking along the street," he said, "and I stopped in front of a topless bar. I wasn't thinking about going inside, I was just tired," the man said, and this got a laugh that also let loose a few sobs. "But I was standing there looking at this . . . establishment, and I felt a hand on my shoulder, and I heard a voice say, 'Ed, you don't want to go in there,' and that voice was coming from Brother Howard Dolan." Everybody nodded and smiled, seemingly satisfied that this summed up my father's life, his kindness and moral stance, but I was astounded that my father, who'd guarded his own feelings and motives so cryptically for his entire life, would have taken it upon himself to openly discuss the motives and feelings of somebody else, particularly while standing out in front of a strip joint.

My father once refused to talk to his older sister Fern for three years. This was during the Depression, in Los Angeles, when they were both, of necessity, living in the same house with their mother. Fern would come and go through the front door, and my father would come and go through the back. My father and mother weren't married yet, though they'd been going together for several years. My mother was a cosmetologist at the beauty shop in the Farmer's Market, in Hollywood, where she frequently caught sight of Lucille Ball at the taco stand; where she once nearly bumped into Clark Gable as he was coming out of the pipe shop; where she cut and permed Robert Taylor's mother's hair; and where she worked with Fern Dolan, who sometimes cried about her brother Howard's cruel silence as she rode to work in the passenger seat of my mother's 1934 Chevy coupe.

My father didn't talk to his brother for twenty years, his oldest daughter for ten.

By this time, three or four years had passed since John had talked to me, and I couldn't help thinking that my brother was keeping up our grim family tradition—silence as a form of punishment—and then I remembered my dog Spike.

When I was fourteen, I got a pit bull terrier from a family who said they "just couldn't handle him anymore." This might also have described the way my parents felt about me. I'd started working at a boarding kennel up the road, and after work I'd smoke pot and drink beer and come home red-eyed and stinking of

Listerine. My parents would concentrate on whatever was in front of them—the TV, a magazine—whenever I floated in. One day, Spike bit a taunting little kid on a tricycle, a couple of tiny holes in one little foot. My father, who knew only the language of authority, made me get rid of the dog. I didn't speak to my father for six months—six months, not one word—and then only after he told me I could get another dog.

Silence as punishment—I realized, as I sat there beside my brother at our father's funeral—was flowing in my veins, too.

The service ended with an organ-and-vocal rendition of "The Old Rugged Cross," and we filed out acting like a family, or how we thought a family should act. We were careful to keep an eye on our mother, who walked unsteadily because of her bad hip. We all spoke softly and kindly to one another, thanked everybody for coming, and displayed a kind of stifled, weary grief that could not entirely conceal the fact that our father's death had been a release for him as well as for us.

There was some sort of postfuneral gathering at Joanne and Ernie's house, which I decided to skip. I drove back to my parents' house, my *mother's* house, where I got out of those funeral clothes as quickly as I could—this was a hot mid-August day in Los Angeles. I put on blue jeans and a T-shirt, then went out to the garage to get something, I don't remember what.

I walked into the garage through the back door, and the coolness of the cement floor felt good under my bare feet. I breathed in the familiar scent of wheel-bearing grease, of motor oil and gasoline, of kerosene and shop rags. I saw an empty glass on the workbench and remembered a summer day in 1963 or 1964, but it could have been almost any day from when I was growing up.

The Oldsmobile was out on the driveway and up on blocks—two big wedges of wood with flattened tops—so the underside of the engine was easier to get to. John's and Dad's legs stuck out from under the car, as if they were large-animal veterinarians doing some kind of field surgery. There was nothing wrong with the Oldsmobile, as far as I could tell, but they were fixing it anyway. They often seemed to be fixing what wasn't broken.

I was out in the front yard. I'd found that by holding a flathead screwdriver by the tip and then sort of whipping it at the ground, I could get the screwdriver to stick in the lawn like a throwing knife. This was an important discovery.

Dad called, "Jay, will you get me a nine-sixteenths box wrench?"

I knew right where the wrenches were. I knew where *everything* was in our garage. The lawn tools were on one side, each tool hanging from its Peg-Board hook (and beneath each hook, penciled in small old-fashioned letters, was the name of the tool meant to hang there: SQUARE-NOSED SHOVEL, ROUND-NOSED SHOVEL, SHORT HOE, LONG HOE, HEDGE CLIPPERS, LEAF RAKE).

The drill press was along the back wall—a big machine, tall as my brother. And along the other wall was the workbench, which was really a number of workbenches. Toward the front was the new workbench John had built; this was where we stored our oil, our gasoline, our power tools. Toward the back there were two old chests of drawers, set about three feet apart and bridged with salvaged plywood and topped with a piece of sheet aluminum; this was the place for close work, whether cleaning a carburetor or fixing a clock. There were two work lights overhead, one up high, the other an old adjustable dining-room lamp that lowered right down on top of your project. Any wrench you might need (or pliers, or vise grips) was in the drawers just below, within easy reach. And on the wall above the chests of drawers were screwdrivers hanging from a little rack on the wall, and next to that was the vinyl pocket that held the punches and chisels and nail sets, and next to that another vinyl pocket with work pencils, pipe cleaners, a tire-pressure gauge, a broken-tipped pocketknife. My father had hammered big finishing nails into the pine boards above this part of the workbench, and from these hung the claw hammer, the tack hammer, the ball peen hammer, the wire brush, the hacksaw, the nail puller, each tool outlined in pencil. These outlines were sort of ghostlike; if you forgot to put a tool back where it belonged, that penciled image would haunt you. Along the rest of the wall were shelves, and on the shelves were jars filled with nuts and bolts and washers, nails and screws. Sometimes, if we had a good earthquake, a few of the jars would fall off and shatter, spilling nuts and bolts, and the floor of the garage would look like an exploded engine.

It felt good to come out of the hot sun and walk into the garage, to feel the cool of the cement underfoot. Sometimes I'd do this and get dizzy; then I'd run back into the sun and do it over again.

I opened the drawer, grabbed a nine-sixteenths wrench.

As I got close to the Oldsmobile, Dad's open, grease-smeared hand extended from underneath. I handed him the wrench, then slid in on the packing blanket next to him to see what he and John were up to.

John held the aluminum-hooded work light so that only what they were working on was lighted; the rest was darkness, shadows, and an occasional spill of yellow light. Dad lifted the wrench to a bolt deep inside the engine. Then he pulled the wrench back out and looked at it closely. *"Box* wrench," he said, and handed me the open-end wrench I'd just given him.

"Oh," I said, and squirmed out from under the Oldsmobile. I got him the nine-sixteenths box wrench, then crawled under the engine again with them. I couldn't see what they were working on. Dad was up to his elbow in engine. John adjusted the work light, maneuvered it deeper into the darkness, and Dad said, "That's it, I can see it now." Dad had reached as far as he could, but John seemed to have a better angle; he hooked the work light on something (I couldn't see him do this but heard the familiar *click*) and without a word took hold of the wrench with Dad, both of them pulling on it for a moment, until there wasn't enough room for two hands, then Dad pulled his hand out and John snugged the bolt tight.

Like the Russian jugglers on *The Ed Sullivan Show,* it was fascinating and exhausting to watch. John and

Dad didn't talk much, but even when they did, I didn't understand the words. *O-ring, flywheel, crankshaft.* I had no idea what they were doing, no idea what they were saying, no idea how one knew when to take hold and the other knew to let go.

I grew sleepy under there, and just as I was nodding off, some specks of road grease fell from the engine onto my face. I squirmed out once again and wandered away, back to the lawn and the sunlight. It occurred to me that I might make the screwdriver stick not only in the lawn but also in the ash tree out front.

I was near to perfecting my throw when Mom came outside with a tray of glasses with lemonade.

"You helping?" Mom said, and I nodded, holding the screwdriver behind my back.

John and Dad stopped for a few minutes and drank the lemonade. They said, "Ah," or "That's good," nothing else, and kept looking at the Oldsmobile, as if it might want to get up and run away. As they lifted their glasses, the muscles in their grease-smeared arms stood out, and I openly stared at them, knowing my arms would never look like that.

John seemed to hear it first, and cocked his head. Then Dad seemed to hear it too. In Dad and John, I could see what I couldn't yet hear. Dad set his empty glass on the workbench, turned to John, and said, "Ford." John, concentrating hard, seemed to agree. Then he said, "With a bad lifter." Just then a car drove past our house. It was a Ford, and a faint ticking was coming from its engine.

In some ways, the garage hadn't changed much since then. One wall, covered with Peg-Board, still held the lawn tools. The drill press was still along the back wall, although it had somehow shrunk. And along the other wall, the workbenches still stretched the whole length of the garage.

During the last ten years, the garage had declined at roughly the same rate as my father's health. My mother's stuff had begun accumulating near the lawn tools, which didn't matter, since a gardener had started coming once a month. There were boxes of old clothes, boxes of yarn, boxes of half-knitted afghans; boxes marked PROJECTS held Styrofoam eggs, artificial flowers, and layer upon layer of fabrics. And there were boxes and boxes of just plain old junk, which my mom seemed to regard as equity for some grand garage sale in the future. It wasn't all her junk. There was junk from Janice, junk from June, dutifully collected by my mother. She'd collected my father's junk, too, such as an IV machine as tall as the drill press, brought home from the hospital after one of my father's near deaths. He'd stopped using the machine some years back, but their insurance had paid for it, so they owned it, just as they owned the several foam-rubber mattress covers, also brought home from the hospital, which now sat moldering and useless on top of the rest of the junk. They couldn't throw anything away. They grew up during the Depression and never got over it. The only difference was that my father had saved stuff he might someday need, and my mother saved stuff she might someday want.

In spite of its order, my father's workbench had never been fussy. He'd kept the sandpaper in an old wooden box with two drawers. He'd hung the gaskets from a nail. The screwdriver holder was an aluminum bracket he'd drilled with different-sized holes and screwed to the wall. Even now, after years of various family members grabbing things and not quite returning them to their rightful places, even strewn with bolts and broken appliances, tipped oil cans and used shop rags, bits of wire and rolls of electrical tape, screwdrivers and pliers and hammers—even with all of this, the workbench still had some sense of order to it, however distressed. I stared at the tool outlines on the wall, and the tool outlines stared back at me.

When I walked back into the house, I was surprised to find John sitting on the sofa reading a newspaper. He didn't look up.

This shouldn't have come as much of a surprise—we were both in town for a few days, him from the Mojave Desert, me from New York City. So even though we seemed to visit our mother in shifts, it was inevitable that we'd run into each other at some point. I walked over, held out my hand, and said, "Hi, John."

John looked up from his newspaper and grudgingly raised his hand. "Hi," he said, or maybe it was "Huh."

Whatever he said, this moment was weirdly formal—shaking hands with my brother like that, after our father's death, after his funeral, after all that we'd been through together. Still, I sat down on the sofa and looked at John as if we were in the middle of a terrifically interesting conversation. I said, "Well, I'm just glad Dad's not suffering anymore."

John had gone back to reading his newspaper, but he looked up and nodded.

I took this as a good sign. I waited for him to say something himself, but he didn't.

"How's the job going?" I said.

This time, John didn't even look up from his newspaper. "Fine," he said.

My neck was stiff from the flight out, where I'd slept with my head pressed against the cabin window, my neck bent as a spoon. I moved my head from side to side, stretching the muscles, and thought of my father's many years of arthritis. And then I said, "I think I'm getting arthritis." I was sort of shocked that I said this. While it wasn't true about me having arthritis, it *could've* been; and true or not, the response would be a good measure of the depth of my brother's anger. "My neck," I said.

But John didn't look at me, and all he said was, "It's probably not arthritis, it'll get better." Then he set his newspaper on the sofa, got out his car keys, and walked out of the house. When he left, he didn't say good-bye or touch the top of the doorway, he just walked out.

I truly hated my brother at that moment, and I hated myself for the shameless ploy, the cheap appeal for sympathy I'd used to even *try* to talk to him. And the kind of bitter loathing I felt after my father's funeral, sitting there alone on my mother's sofa with a flushed face, was close to what I felt when I woke up with a stiff neck on a low-budget, overbooked flight from Paris, on my way to a burn unit in Phoenix, on my way to John's survival or death or funeral—I had no idea what lay ahead.

I woke up over the Pacific and saw out my window the smog-filled Los Angeles Basin. The plane went into a steep, wrong-feeling descent, and it was only then that I noticed the extraordinary shabbiness of the overhead compartments, the seats, even the wing outside my window; everything seemed to be shaking, worn-out, and cheap. I remember thinking that only an act of God could get this winged junkyard safely on the ground—as only an act of God could have gotten us this far. And then I remember thinking that if we crashed, somebody would probably attribute this to God's will, too—*so mote it be*—even if we crashed and burned.

But we landed, somehow—a rough landing with several big bounces, the whole plane going into a kind of epileptic fit, and all the passengers leaning back in their seats with their heels pressed forward. As the plane slowed on the runway, some of them emitted muffled, birdlike screams. A few of the drunker passengers cheered.

I did neither.

Ernie was waiting for me at the boarding gate. My nephews weren't with him this time, and I sort of wished they were. I'd expected to hear Ernie say the same thing all over again—*I'm sorry, Jay, you almost made it*—and in some ways I was disappointed when he didn't.

"How you doin', Jay?" he said, and put his hand on my shoulder. "So, how was Paris?"

I took a deep breath and waited for him to go on.

"No change," he said.

On the drive home, Ernie told me the latest news about the blast. John's condition was critical but stable. Another man had died. "Some of the others probably won't make it, either," Ernie said, and looked at me. I knew from the way he said this that one of the others was John. "I was there yesterday, Jay, in Phoenix." Ernie bit his lip, shook his head. "I didn't even recognize him."

"Jesus," I said.

"It's fucking unbelievable," Ernie said.

It was past rush hour and Ernie drove his Porsche fast, not recklessly but sneakily—never signaling, and sometimes passing on the right instead of the left. In driving and in life, Ernie tended to ignore certain fundamental rules.

As we headed east on the Santa Monica Freeway, I stared at the Hollywood Hills with the dumb fascination of a just-arrived tourist, which, to some extent, I was. I'd been in Paris only a few weeks, but I'd lived in New York now for years. With every return to Los Angeles I felt a little more detached, a little more foreign—although I'd also felt detached and foreign when I lived here, so in that sense, at least, I felt at home.

During the years when most sensible people go to college, I'd lived in Hollywood and worked in the music business—a combination that strikes me now, from the safe distance of twenty years, as hilarious.

It didn't seem so hilarious as I rode in the car with my brother-in-law that evening. That life was still too close, too real, too much at odds with the new life I fancied for myself.

The night I'd made the decision to become a writer, I was working as a tour manager for Cher—who at the time wasn't a movie star, just a famous pop relic with a big Vegas production. I'd been on the road with different musical groups for five years, mostly rock 'n' roll bands, working first as a roadie and then as a tour manager, and I found myself, at twenty-three, staring at a white TV in the dressing room of Caesar's Tahoe. Or maybe it was Caesar's Palace. I'd been on the road long enough that every place seemed the same. But the TV was white, I remember that. Everything in the dressing room was white: white couch, white carpeting, white piano. I sat on the white couch and stared at the white TV and clicked the remote control from one channel to the next, my arm outstretched like a boy holding a make-believe sword.

The show was going on downstairs. I'd never actually watched the spectacle from beginning to end, but I'd witnessed it plenty of times in pieces, all the way from rehearsals in Hollywood to its first run at Caesar's Palace in Las Vegas.

I was in charge of an entourage of forty-five people: musicians, technicians, backup singers, dancers, drag queens (one did Diana Ross, another did Bette Midler), a wig stylist, a masseuse, a dresser, and sometimes there were Cher's kids, Cher's kids' friends, Cher's sister, Cher's boyfriend, Cher's choreographer, Cher's choreographer's boyfriend, Cher's hairstylist. And me. Actually, there was very little for me to be in charge of, since a show like this would go up for a month, and everybody went about their jobs with the regularity of factory workers.

I'd done up our itinerary with Cher's glitzy CHER logo, and then under it I'd taken the Ralph Steadman lettering from Hunter S. Thompson's *Fear and Loathing in Las Vegas,* so it read CHER . . . IN LAS VEGAS, and under that was Steadman's hellish drawing of Raoul Duke and his lawyer on the way to Las Vegas in their Great Red Shark. Some of the entourage remarked that the itinerary looked odd.

The guitar player started the twangy intro to a song called "Those Shoes" and I changed the channel. This was the part of the show where Cher was wheeled across

49

the darkened stage on top of a giant high-heeled shoe, and I knew this had been accomplished because when the spotlights hit Cher, sitting monstrous and imperial in the heel, the whole audience gasped. I changed the channel. Next, Cher slid down the instep and popped out of the open toe, and the six dancers picked her up and carried her around the stage in the sort of ritual usually involving a trussed pig. The audience applauded wildly, and I changed the channel again.

I had a sudden vision of myself watching TV in a tacky dressing room in Las Vegas or Lake Tahoe or wherever the hell I was, and then it struck me that this wasn't a vision: this was me, this was my life. I didn't know how long I'd been sitting there. I didn't know what I was going to do next. But I did know that I had to do something, because it occurred to me, with great clarity, that I hated my life.

At about this same time, it had occurred to my brother that he also hated my life.

" . . . and I'm telling you, Jay, I wouldn't wish that on *anybody*."

"What's that?" I said.

"Not on anybody," Ernie said.

I wasn't exactly sure what Ernie was talking about, but figured he was talking about the blast, and if it *did* have to be wished on somebody, the somebody he'd wish it on was John.

"What if he lives?" I said.

"Nightmare," Ernie said, and looked at me, waiting for my lead.

"If he was pissed off at the world before," I said, "what would he be like after this?"

"Tell me about it," Ernie said. "The fucking guy. Pissed off at everybody. You. Me. Your sister. How long's it been since he talked to you?"

I couldn't precisely say when John had stopped talking to me. For the first year or so, I didn't even notice. Some hint of my life on the road. Still, when I did notice, I was indignant; and to make it worse, I had to be indignant in retrospect. I shrugged and said, "Four years . . . five."

I didn't like being back in Los Angeles and I didn't like this conversation, either. I didn't like being in collusion with Ernie, but I was.

We'd driven past downtown Los Angeles and were now on the Pomona Freeway, which ran a few hundred yards from my parents' house. When the freeway was being built, I'd sneaked out at night and moved the surveyors' stakes. I didn't want a freeway messing up the hills I liked to romp in. But I finally gave up, and the freeway was finished, and in time became useful. In the months before it opened, I rode my bicycle on it, perfecting my wheelies in the passing lane. And after it opened, I'd watch the aftermath of gruesome crashes at the off-ramp across from our backyard. The highway patrol cars, the ambulances and fire engines and wreckers—it was lit up like Christmas over there. Sometimes I'd hear the crash and see it right after it happened. I'd stand on the wobbly picnic table in our backyard with my dog, Tiger, howling soulfully beside me. I'd hear the sirens in the distance. I'd watch the dust and smoke rising from the crumpled metal that used to be a car, its wheels still spinning.

"If he lives," Ernie said, "he'll be a . . ."

"A monster," I said.

. . .

The thought of being at my mom's house by myself seemed spooky, so I stayed at Joanne and Ernie's house that night. Besides, Joanne had flown home to check on her kids, and she and I were going to catch the first flight out, the next morning, to Phoenix.

My mother's house was the same house I was raised in, the same house my brother and sisters were raised in. It was a three-bedroom, one-bath tract house that seemed to be getting smaller year by year. In the back-yard, the clothesline wires had drooped at roughly the same rate that my mother had become shorter.

Joanne and Ernie's house wasn't far away, but it was bigger and in a better neighborhood. My mom's house was on one side of some hills, with views of a gas station, a freeway, a dump. Joanne and Ernie's neighborhood was on the other side of those hills, and had views of big houses, wide streets, and ivy.

To walk into their house was always sort of disorient-ing, since my sister redecorated the house more or less constantly. In the front of the house was a largely unused semiformal living room that had the look and warmth of a furniture showcase. Ernie set my bags down near the door and we both looked into the immaculate living room for a moment, and he waited until I'd said the obligatory "Hmm, nice" before taking me back to the family room, formerly the pool room, where Joanne had evidently discovered country French.

It was late. My niece and nephews were already asleep. Joanne had made a bed for me on the couch, but I was so exhausted from the trip I could have slept on a coffee table. I got out of my clothes, got under the covers.

Ernie came into the family room and said, "Need anything, Jay?" He was holding something behind his back.

"No, I'm fine, thanks."

"A drink or anything?"

"No, really, I'm fine, I'm already asleep."

"Something to read?"

Just then, Joanne made an appearance. She was wearing a white satin bathrobe, and though it was late at night, she looked startlingly fresh and present, like some kind of suburban Kabuki dancer. Many years later, after their divorce, she told me with some dismay that she used to put on makeup for Ernie before she went to bed.

"Hi, hon," she said. She came over to the couch and gave me a hug. She smelled like the perfume counter at Bloomingdale's.

"Hi, Jo," I said.

"Need anything, hon?" she said.

"I'm fine," I said.

"We'll talk in the morning," she said.

I nodded.

"Are you *sure* you don't want to read yourself to sleep?" Ernie said, and handed me what he'd been holding behind his back.

It was a comic book, something that probably belonged to my nephew Michael, who was just entering (we would later find out) a particularly brutal period of his life. I didn't get it at first, the comic book, and then looked closer. On the cover, sneering, ready to lunge, was a villain—a monster, really—his skin a patchwork of deep scars. The scars of somebody who'd been burned.

Ernie was grinning at his inside joke. Our joke.

"Oh, Ernie," Joanne said playfully.

"Good night, Jay," he said.

Joanne smiled, snugged the covers to my chest.

A few days earlier, I'd felt as if my life was moving forward, but now I felt as if I'd been dragged back—way back—to a part of my life I'd worked hard to leave behind. Back here, I was a little kid again. Back here, I was terrified by monsters, terrified of the dark. Back here, I was a little boy whose big sister—*Good night, hon*—tucked him sweetly into bed.

"It doesn't look like him," Joanne said. She'd already told me this when we had coffee that morning in her kitchen, the house quiet and the windows dark. She'd said it as she drove us to the airport in her white Jaguar, and she said it again now, as our commuter flight gained altitude at an angle that reminded me of the old wooden roller coaster on the pier at P.O.P.—Pacific Ocean Park, in Santa Monica—where Joanne had taken me for my seventh birthday, and where, shortly after that roller-coaster ride, I'd thrown up. "It doesn't look like him," she said. "So be prepared."

Pressed back into my seat, I gripped the armrests. "Uh-huh," I said, and felt my ears pop.

I turned and looked out the window at the blue sky above, the brown smog below. I kept edging closer to the glass as the smog cleared and the suburbs gave way to desert, and soon I was hunched at the little window, staring down at the vast and barren geography of my family.

My parents were born and raised in the Imperial Valley in California, which is an irrigated desert. The water was stolen from the Colorado River via the All-American Canal, which some of my mother's brothers helped build. My mother's family—Uncle Olin and Aunt Laura Jean, Uncle Laurie and Aunt Izzy, Uncle Benny and Aunt Helen—used to visit us with the dust from the stockyards or the sugar-beet fields still on their boots, the trunks of their dusty Fords loaded with the lettuce and cantaloupes and onions they'd brought for us and claimed to have stolen, their field-tan faces working hard not to laugh at the thought—a laugh because the Derricks knew everybody in El Centro and were welcome to trunk-harvest whatever they wanted. My mother's family had come to the Imperial Valley from Texas, and my grandfather, Anderson Bradford Derrick, was considered one of its pioneers. He never acquired much wealth, though he did acquire many kids. He had one small farm or ranch after another, making a little money with each sale, and for many years was the tax collector and the president of the historical society. My mother's family loved the desert, loved farming and farming stories, and stories about ranches, and animals, and swimming in irrigation ditches, and stories about earthquakes—of which there were some big ones. They liked to tell stories about when the writer Harold Bell Wright came to the Imperial Valley and lived in a little shack alongside their farm while working on his novel *The Winning of Barbara Worth*.

My father's family, the Dolans—his mother, Stella, and his sisters, Lucille and Fern—had moved to Los Angeles to get away from the desert. These women, also originally from Texas, wore pleated gabardine dresses with severe shoulders and feather-trimmed hats. They were sour-lipped and hard-eyed, their skin as pale as the cotton doilies they often crocheted. They didn't want to admit or remember the squalor of the Imperial Valley during the Depression. Instead, they collected teacups and, except in anger, said "isn't" instead of "ain't." They were city ladies now, and seldom even said the name of their hometown, Brawley. For them, the desert was as dark and mysterious as the blood orchids they wore on their wide lapels.

Joanne was born in Yuma, Arizona—a little desert town alongside the Colorado River and now and then the hottest place on earth—when my father was stationed there at the army airfield at the end of World War II. John was conceived in Yuma just before my mother and father moved back to Los Angeles, where he and the rest of us were born—and Los Angeles, too, beneath its freeways and streets and overwatered lawns, is a desert. Sometimes when the Santa Ana winds were blowing, big tumbleweeds would drift across our lawn.

The desert could be hot enough to fry an egg on a sidewalk, and cold enough to kill a lettuce crop in a single freeze. My father said he'd seen both and would never forget it. The desert was vast and powerful, mysterious and silent, and in this way it seemed to hold secrets. It could be sweet and it could be deadly, it could be loved and it could be hated, but the desert could not be forgotten. It was part of us, and we were part of it.

The sun was bright on the horizon, and the window beside my seat was getting hot. I lowered the plastic shade and said to Joanne, "You know, I don't even know why he stopped talking to me."

Joanne closed her copy of *House Beautiful* and gave me a sincere I-feel-your-pain look.

I'd hoped for more. I didn't really want her to feel my pain, but to give me a clue. I wanted to know why my brother was so pissed off in general and why, in particular, at me. I figured Joanne, being the oldest, would have an intuitive sense of where it had all started, or, better yet, that she'd have hard facts.

"Isn't that weird?" I said. "Him never even telling me?"

Joanne put the magazine in the seat pocket in front of her and said, "He's a Dolan."

"But five years?" I said.

Joanne, uncharacteristically, shrugged. "Dad didn't talk to me for *ten* years."

I knew—thought I knew—what Joanne was talking about. She'd gotten engaged to Ernie when she was twenty-one, and because Ernie was a Mexican-American, my father, in a fine display of racism, refused to walk his oldest daughter down the aisle—refused to even attend the wedding. He didn't relent until sometime after she'd had her third child. Still, the years didn't add up.

"Ten years?" I said. "Because of Ernie?"

"Ernie was part of it," Joanne said. "But it started with the Thunderbird."

I smiled at the memory of Joanne coming home with that car. We were all sitting in the living room watching TV when she pulled up—it was sleek and white and loaded with chrome—and she parked in the shade of the ash tree, right behind John's red Corvette. (John never parked under the ash tree, for fear of bird shit on his red leather seats.)

Joanne, with her beehive hairdo, had to angle her head to get out of the car, but once that was done she emerged waving and smiling like the Queen of the Rose Parade. She must have known we'd all be watching.

Janice, who had a semibeehive hairdo herself, shoved June aside and flung the screen door open; then she did a kind of hurried stroll across the lawn.

June jumped up and down in front of the TV—"Joanne got a new car! Joanne got a new car!"—and then was out the door herself.

Mom came into the living room from the kitchen, said, "Oh," and smiled.

Dad lowered his newspaper and looked out the window. He said, "What the . . ." His mouth was open. He blinked a few times.

John finished the glass of milk he was drinking, then got up and walked outside as if he was simply checking to see if his Corvette was all right. He often checked to see if his Corvette was all right.

I walked out with John and said, "Wow!" then looked up to see if he would wow back.

Joanne was standing beside her Thunderbird, smiling.

"Sixty-two?" John said.

"Yep," Joanne said. "Not even twenty thousand miles. The salesman called it a 'cream puff.' "

John's face went into a minor sneer. He was distrustful of salesmen, salesmen's promises, promises in general. He kept his hands shoved into the back pockets of his Levi's as he worked his way around the car, inspecting but not touching it. Joanne lifted the hood so he could sniff around the engine.

The Thunderbird was low-slung and graceful-looking, with a silver-blue interior and a dashboard that looked like a cockpit from a rocket ship. Even at eight, I somehow knew that the Thunderbird had something to do with sex.

Janice stared into the car's passenger window as if into a crystal ball.

June was still jumping up and down. "It's really beautiful!" she said.

John took his hands out of his back pockets. Then he raised his hands and took hold of the hood right near the chrome Thunderbird in the middle. He brought the hood down slowly and shut it with an authoritative *shunk*. We were all watching, and when John nodded and said, "Pretty clean," it sounded like a blessing.

Joanne looked as if she'd just won a blue ribbon. "Want to go for a ride?" she said to us, and it was a scramble for the shotgun seat. Janice and June almost got into another of their tiffs, but Joanne mediated by telling Janice that she could ride in front first and June that she could ride in front on the way back. I shoved my hands into the back pockets of my Levi's and went into an instant sulk—until Joanne leaned down and whispered, "And how about a snow cone for you?"

John was walking toward his Corvette, and Joanne said, "Hey, John."

He stopped, turned.

"Thanks," she said.

John's face went into a minor sneer again, but this time it had a smile on top of it.

Our father, however, was not smiling. He'd wanted Joanne to buy a good sound transportation car—a Rambler sedan, a Dodge Dart. To him it didn't matter that she was twenty-one, working full-time, and had paid for the car herself. Nor did it matter to him that John, who was two years younger than Joanne, had just bought himself a red Corvette. That was different. Joanne was his daughter, and she lived in his home, and she therefore would have to live by his rules.

On the flight, Joanne turned to me and said, "And when I came home past my curfew one night, that was it."

"You had a curfew?" I said.

"Didn't you?" Joanne said.

I shook my head. I thought of a story my mom liked to tell when I was growing up. She'd say how she used to put me in a room with my toys, and then a few hours later she'd think, *Oh my god, I forgot about him!* Then she'd say how she'd come running back and fling the door open, and there I'd be, thoroughly engrossed—my mom actually used those words, "thoroughly engrossed"—in my toys, playing quietly and happily by myself.

My mom meant this to mean that I was a good boy.

Joanne didn't say anything for a minute, but we were probably thinking the same thing—how we'd both had the same mother and the same father, yet been raised by very different parents.

My father told Joanne that if she wasn't going to live by his rules, she'd have to move out of his house—and no doubt to his amazement, she did.

Our house got very quiet the next few days, as Joanne packed her boxes and carried them out to her Thunderbird.

We were all sitting in the living room, Dad reading the newspaper and the rest of us watching TV, when Joanne carried out the last of her things. From his La-Z-Boy Dad said "Sis?" and it seemed as if he was going to wish her well, tell her to be careful, offer to help her if she needed it.

Joanne was holding one last box with both hands. She turned expectantly and said, "Yes?"

"You know the hours I work and the days I'm home. Don't be here when I'm here."

With the box trembling in her hands, Joanne nodded and said, "Okay, I won't," and Dad barely but noticeably flinched.

The rest of us sat stunned in front of the TV while Joanne walked out of our lives—or at least our lives together. Our father raised his newspaper in front of him, and from what Joanne was telling me, he stayed behind it, in silence, for the next ten years.

"And it ended when Michael was born," I said.

"No, Dad . . . *tolerated* me after that. He'd say hello and how are you doing and good-bye, and he was always good to Michael, and later to Lisa and Jeff, but we didn't really talk until after he got out of the hospital, after that first heart attack."

I was stunned. *Hello, how are you doing, good-bye.* To me, with my father, that *was* really talking.

After Joanne moved out, our house became pressurized by our father's silence. Sometimes a door would mysteriously slam shut, and though common sense told me it was just the wind, I always jumped. I could feel the pressure as soon as he came home from work and opened the front door, or when he sat in the La-Z-Boy and read the newspaper, or when he clicked open his Zippo lighter and lit a Chesterfield King. He never raised his voice and he never mentioned Joanne's name. He hadn't exactly banished her from the house, only when he was there. Still, he'd sentenced her to a kind of exile, which came in the form of silence; and with this sentence, he'd also silenced himself.

And the rest of us. Joanne and John had taught me to read, so I hid between the covers of books, flat as a page. My mother cooked. Janice and June fought with each other, although Janice managed to maintain some kind of stubborn connection with our father. John stayed away—and answered our father's silence with his own.

Our plane banked in its descent into Phoenix. I lifted the plastic shade and looked out the window.

"And it's been two years now since John talked to me," Joanne said.

"What?" I said, turning to look at her.

"Two years," she said. She seemed surprised that I was surprised.

The parking lot of the Maricopa County Medical Center is all heat and light. The sunlight comes down on you like a great soft weight, comes reflecting at you sideways off of every car, comes *up* at you from the gummy asphalt—you can feel its heat through the soles of your shoes—while everything in the distance is a shimmering liquid, and the distance in front of you is the burn unit.

At the entrance to the burn unit you step on a black rubber mat and the automatic doors wheeze open with a blast of cold air and then you're walking down a long dark hallway and somehow you always knew you'd be doing this, not just walking down a hallway but walking down this *exact* hallway, with these fluorescent lights overhead giving off a cold hard light, with the linoleum cold and hard underneath your feet. Every corner and every surface looks cold and hard, even the few chairs and the sofa along the wall, and even the doctor who walks past manages only a cold hard smile and your body replies with a little epileptic shiver and you walk on.

There's a warning sign on the wide door at the end of the hallway, BURN UNIT, NO UNAUTHORIZED PERSONS, and I open the door for my sister not to be polite but so she'll go in first.

We're greeted by a pretty nurse who smiles and says hello, and I feel guilty for noticing that the nurse is pretty and for probably acting however it is I act when I get around a pretty woman.

"You know the routine," the pretty nurse says to Joanne, "you can take him through it," then strides off in her white shoes.

"Through what?" I whisper.

Joanne turns on the water at the little sink near the door and washes her hands, then begins suiting up: paper slippers, paper smock, paper cap, and a paper surgeon's mask that covers half her face. All of it is baby blue.

I do the same, and I'm grateful as I shuffle in my slippers down the hallway of the burn unit, because what flares up from my heart is pure fear, but what shows on my face is paper and baby blue. I snug my surgeon's mask a little higher.

Even with all of Joanne's warnings, I still don't know what to expect, and I find myself not so much shuffling as *creeping* down the hallway, as if ready for some monster to jump out and bite me on the neck. But the burn unit is utterly calm, and this calmness is unnerving. One nurse sits behind a counter, writing something. Another nurse (the pretty one) walks by and smiles. A doctor stands nearby, reading a chart.

Each patient's room has a big open doorway that faces the nurses' station, and as I look inside the first room my legs go heavy and numb.

There's a body lying in the bed. Though it seems to be a man's body, there's nothing familiar about it. The arms are bandaged but the face is exposed, a face swollen and splotched red and black, and it doesn't look like my brother but it reminds me of somebody, of something, except right now I can't think of what. Then it—*he*—turns and looks at me, and I hurry to the next door, grateful once again for my surgeon's mask.

The body in the next room is worse, although my notions of better and worse are evolving rapidly. This body—it looks to be a man's from the size of it—is also bandaged around the arms, but the face is even more swollen, more burned, and the stiffness of the arms suggests that the rest of the body is as badly burned as the face—a face as red, I can't help thinking, as a lobster. The body is hooked up to an array of machines and IVs, and the drip of the IVs and the flicker of the machines are the only things moving in the room. I look closely at the body, I stare at it, without recognizing a thing—nothing.

I look into the third room, the fourth, and the sameness more than the burns is what gets me. The bandaged arms, the swollen faces, the skin reddened and yellowed and blackened and distorted—to me, all the burn victims look alike. And, dressed in baby blue from head to foot, all the visitors probably do too. I ask Joanne if she knows where John is, and she points to the second room I looked in. I look again at the swollen, bloodred body. I stare at it. Still unrecognizable. But that's John, she's telling me. That's what's left of our brother.

Joanne rests one hand on my shoulder as we go into the room—a small gesture to help steady me, and it does—but I can tell that it's also to help steady herself.

The IV bags drip. The machines near the bed display blips and jagged lines in green flashes. They mean something, and I'm not sure I want to find out what.

When I was little and overwhelmed by something, Joanne would calm me with her presence and help me find the words I was struggling for. And as we stood beside that hospital bed, beside a body I'd been told was my brother's, I was, at twenty-eight, suddenly little and overwhelmed again. And Joanne, at forty, was once again my big sister.

"Hi, John," she said loudly—she'd told me earlier that he'd be heavily drugged and that his hearing might have been damaged in the blast. "We're here. It's Joanne and Jay. We're here. I love you."

I tried to think of what John would do if he was standing here and I was in that bed, and I thought of how he'd probably tell me things were going to be okay, tell me to keep going, be strong, everything's going to be okay—but I couldn't manage any of that. I couldn't even think of anything to say, and couldn't have said it if I had.

I was sobbing, and Joanne was sobbing, and her sobbing made mine worse. She looked at me and said softly, "Go ahead."

The doctors would later describe his wounds as "a huge insult to his system," and at that moment I was beginning to see exactly that. His hair was matted and had been lopped off in places. I could see marks on his forehead from adhesive tape. There were oxygen tubes in his nose. A dry catheter was connected to his penis, and large IV needles were jabbed into the big veins near his groin. His legs were exposed, as was the side of his body. I could see the neat line where his work boot had ended at his ankle, and less distinct lines that had marked the top and bottom of his underwear. Those were the only areas of his skin that he'd have left—if he lived.

The best I could get out was a whimper. I said, "Hi, John. It's Jay." Saying "Hi" to my brother after what he'd gone through, and after the years of silence between us, felt terrifically inadequate. I tried to say "I'm sorry" and I tried to say "I love you," but what came out was more whimpering. And then, because I was whimpering so much and didn't know what else to say, I used the words Joanne had just helped me with. I coughed and then said, clearly, "We're here. We're here."

John opened his eyes—even his eyelids were swollen—and lifted his head maybe an inch from the pillow, his whole body shaking from the effort. I looked at the panicked urgency in his eyes—that's when I knew for sure that this was John—and then at the display on one of the machines, as if it could tell me of my brother's anger even if my brother could not.

A nurse had come in to check something, and as John moved his lips and struggled to speak, the nurse cheerfully explained his difficulty: "His throat is burned too."

"*It's okay, John,*" Joanne said.

But something wasn't okay, and John struggled with everything in him to be understood. He was shaking just trying to say the words, moving his lips, but no sound came out.

Joanne said, *"I know you do, I know you do. It's okay."*

John nodded, closed his eyes, and let his head fall back against the pillow. That effort—lifting his head, moving his lips—had exhausted him. The nurse began prepping him for surgery, and as she gently lifted his arm, his whole body went electric with pain.

"You'd better go now," the nurse said to us. "We'll have him back in a little while."

Joanne nodded to the nurse. *"We love you, John,"* she said, and with my rising and inarticulate grief, I said—or tried to say—the same thing.

Before leaving the burn unit, we had to take off and throw away our baby blue garments, which I found out later were partly to protect John, and partly to protect us. The explosion had been a deadly combination of superheated steam and the asbestos particles that had covered the pipe—a pipe about as big around as a manhole cover, with walls more than an inch thick. Those asbestos particles were imbedded in his skin, his throat, his lungs.

I pulled off my surgeon's mask and said, "He was trying to say something to us."

Joanne nodded.

I said, "It was something like, 'I want you know . . . ' or 'I want you both . . . ' Jesus, I wonder if he wanted *both* of us to get out."

Joanne pulled off her surgeon's mask and looked at me.

When I walked from the burn unit into the waiting room, I felt naked without my baby blue protective garments. I could feel the glaring presence of myself, my clothes, my ability to stand and breathe and walk. I breathed deep, put on my best man-of-the-family face, and walked to where my mom and my other sisters were sitting like wounded birds.

"Did he say anything?" Janice said.

Joanne nodded yes.

I didn't believe her, but said nothing.

My mother asked me how my trip had been, and this saddened me beyond all reason. It didn't seem fair, now, that I'd been vacationing in Europe when this had happened to John, and that my life was moving forward even as we spoke. It didn't seem fair to be alive.

"Is your article out yet?" my mother said.

"Story," I said. "No, not yet." I was at once proud and ashamed—proud that my first story was being published, and ashamed that, as my brother lay dying, I could still feel such pride.

Then we sat there saying nothing, my mother, my three sisters, and I, in a waiting room that wasn't even a room but a corridor with stiff chairs, a stiff couch, and a coffee table. We stared at the pilled fabric on the couch. We stared at the scuff marks on the hospital linoleum. Above us, the fluorescent lights hummed. There were automatic doors with tinted glass at the front of the waiting room, and each time they slid open, letting in a spill of sunlight and soft heat, we looked hopefully in that direction, as if the answer to our prayers might somehow arrive on foot.

One of my brother's friends, Al Laven, sat in the waiting room with us, diligent as any family member—maybe more. He and John had gone through training together at Southern California Edison's Mohave Generating Station, in Laughlin, Nevada, across the Colorado River from Bullhead City, Arizona. For the last year and a half they'd studied together, worked together, become friends. "Just last week," Al said, "John was baby-sitting my kids."

We all said the same sort of thing, in numbness and disbelief: *Just a few days ago . . . last week . . . last month . . .*

I had to go back a bit further.

"John's a great guy," Al said. "I know he's going to make it."

My mother was seventy, small and white-haired. She walked with a limp. A year later, when her hip would be replaced, the surgeon would add an inch and a half of metal to replace what had worn down in bone. She nodded at Al with weary optimism.

"John's *real*," Al said. "He's the kind of guy you can really talk to."

My mouth twisted into something like a smile.

"And he's great with the kids," Al said.

I stared at him. Al was tall and thin, his tan face raccooned from sunglasses, his dark hair shaped by the SOUTHERN CALIFORNIA EDISON baseball cap he now held in his hands. He looked to be in his mid-thirties— about halfway in years between me and John—and because of this, he seemed to fit in with my family in ways that I never had and never would. I was the youngest of the bunch. Joanne had changed my diapers, read me stories, taught me my first words. John and I had shared a bedroom; when I was little and waking from bad dreams, he'd tell me, from the lower bunk, "It's okay." John had taught me how to throw a ball, bait a hook, sight a rifle. He'd taught me how to ride a motor-cycle and drive a stick shift. I'd known my brother for twenty-eight years—most of his life and all of mine. True, he hadn't talked to me for five years, but those earlier years counted for something, although just then I wasn't sure what. But now this good friend, this good man, this Al Laven who'd worked with him for a good goddamn year and a half was sitting there telling me who my brother was. I turned away while he went on talking, but I still listened.

Al Laven knew the circumstances of the blast and the condition of all sixteen victims, who were defined less by who they were than by what they had lost, or would soon lose—90, 80, 60 percent of their skin. He told us that two men had already died. Most of the others, he told us, had been airlifted to a burn unit in

Las Vegas, though one man had gone to Long Beach, a woman to Salt Lake City. He drew elaborate diagrams for us, with penciled slashes to show where the reheat pipe had failed. He explained to us what a reheat pipe was, and what failure, in this sense, meant. He told us of the rescue efforts after the blast, the confusion and heroism and panic: how the whole community had mobilized; how trucks, bringing ice to pack the wounds, had come from as far away as Kingman, and how helicopters had flown in from all over the West. He told us how much John liked his job, how much John loved the desert—how John had, in fact, put a down payment on a lot in Bullhead City, not far from Al's house. He gave testimony to the excellence of my brother's character and offered to lead us in prayer.

Al Laven knew everything, it seemed—the blast, my brother, even Jesus. Once I actually joined hands with him and prayed, although I imagine our prayers were not the same.

"I know John's going to make it," Al said to Joanne. "I just know he is."

Joanne was forty and had three children of her own, but here, with us, she was still our big sister, with a big sister's reserve and self-possession, and a kindness tempered with wisdom. She looked at Al and smiled sadly.

"That's right!" Janice, the middle sister, said. "He's going to make it!" She said this not so much as part of the conversation but as a challenge to all comers, especially our mother.

Al leaned forward, as if ready to let us in on a secret. He said, "Last time I was in there, I think he could hear me."

"What?" June said. She was the second youngest, seven years older than me. "What?" She had been brooding, and fading in and out of sleep. Her face was puffy from crying, and one cheek was crosshatched from pressing into the couch's sturdy fabric.

"I knew it!" Janice said.

"What?" June said.

"Yeah," Al said. "I was saying to him, 'Hey, buddy, you've *got* to make it—who else am I going to get to baby-sit my kids?' " Al grinned and said, "I'm pretty sure his arm moved."

Whatever we hoped for John—a medical miracle or a swift death—had to do with how much he could hear, how much he could feel, and, if he could speak to us, what he would say. Those were profound issues, but all I could think of just then was that Al Laven had the right to call my brother "buddy" and I didn't.

The first time I'd ever been to a hospital was to see my uncle Chet. Until a few days earlier, I didn't even know I *had* an Uncle Chet, didn't know my father had a brother or, if I did know about it, figured he was dead. Most everybody in my father's family was ancient or dead.

My father drove the Oldsmobile and my mother sat in the passenger seat. I sat in the middle of the backseat, leaning forward. Those were our regular places—my father on my left, my mother on my right, and me resting my chin on their seat and looking at my father's fixed expression in the rearview mirror. There was a Dopp kit on the front seat between them, though I wasn't sure why my father had brought it.

As we were walking into the hospital I said, "Do I call him Uncle Chester or Uncle Chet?"

My father tucked the Dopp kit under his arm, took a deep breath, and walked into the hospital.

"Just tell him hello," my mother said.

In the hospital room there was a bed with a dark fat man in it. He wasn't just fat—he looked swollen. His fingers were like sausages, and so were his lips. I was surprised and a little scared when he turned and looked at us. "Hello, Howard," he said.

"Hello, Chet. You remember Arlie."

"Good to see you, Chet," my mother said. Then she nudged me forward. "And this is J.D."

"J.D.?" Chet said.

I'd gone through this routine for as long as I could remember. I stepped forward and said, "It's my real name. J period D period. On my birth certificate. It doesn't stand for anything."

"Oh it doesn't, does it?" Chet looked at my father. "J.D., huh?" he said, and started laughing and then coughing.

"Need anything?" my father said.

"I could use a drink," he said.

My father bit his lip, then went into a big production of pouring some water into a paper cup beside the bed. The production seemed directed toward me—I wasn't sure why—but even I knew that water wasn't what Chet meant when he said he could use a drink.

My father held the paper cup to Chet's fat lips and Chet sipped a little and coughed some more. Water dribbled down his stubbled chin. "All right," he said, "all right."

"Feeling okay?" my father said. "Everything all right?"

"Hell, I don't know," Chet said. Then he looked at me and said, "What are *you* looking at?"

I stood up quickly. I'd been leaning forward and looking under the sheet. My friend Jerry Dunlap had whispered to me at recess that my *thing* was going to get *huge* as soon as I turned thirteen, and I'd told him it already did that almost every night, and he'd said, no, huge *all* the time. And this wasn't just anybody talking—this was *Jerry Dunlap*. So in the hospital I wasn't trying to be a pervert, I was just looking under the sheet to try and get a peek at the future.

Chet said, "You're looking at my feet, aren't you?" Then he sort of sang, "Old feet . . . feet, feet, feet."

I wasn't sure which was worse, sneaking a look at his thing or sneaking a look at his feet. His feet were gross. I put my hands in my pockets and tried to smile.

"Well, you'd probably feel better if you had a shave," my father said, and set the Dopp kit on the table beside the bed.

"A what?"

"You'll feel better."

"No, Howard, really . . ."

"I don't mind."

I knew that Chet didn't mean, *No, don't bother,* he meant, *No. Really.* And I knew my father knew this too.

Chet let out a deep breath.

"No trouble at all," my father said, and unzipped the Dopp kit.

The thick white shaving cream looked funny on Chet's dark skin—like the fake beards Santa Clauses always wear. My father ran the razor down Chet's face, a sound like paper tearing.

"I'll be down in the gift shop," my mother said, and Chet lifted one hand as if he wanted her to pull him out of there.

I gave her a look that meant the same thing.

"I'll leave you boys alone," she said.

Chet lowered his hand the way dead people do in the movies.

I sat down in the hard metal chair near the bed.

My father scraped away another swath of shaving cream. "You know, Mother's still alive, even though you hadn't thought to ask. She'll be here in a while, her and Lucille."

"Oh yeah? Careful."

"Sorry."

"I guess . . . I guess it's good."

"You guess?"

"Aw, hell, Howard, I don't know."

My father always called his mother "Mother"—he never called her "Mom" or "my mother." I don't know why, but my father saying Mother this and Mother that always gave me the creeps; of course my grandmother always gave me the creeps anyway, no matter what you called her.

My grandmother was always Monnie to me. She'd gotten that name from John when he was little and tried to call her Mommy and couldn't pronounce it. For some reason I could never figure out, the name stuck. Monnie was ancient, and her ancient daughter, my aunt Lucille, lived with her. They had a way of saying hello that made it sound like a complaint. I could hear them out in the hallway asking for Chester Dolan's room.

And then the room was suddenly all Monnie and Lucille, all gabardine dresses and black lace hats and the stench of their orchid corsages. I tried to make myself blend into the hard metal chair.

My father wiped Chet's face with a wet towel, then dabbed at a spot on his chin with a styptic pencil. The spot bloomed like a tiny rose. "There you go, buddy."

To hear my father say *buddy* was weird, since Chet didn't really seem like one.

"OH MY!" said Monnie or Lucille. "OH LORD!"

My father stood back and looked at Chet the same way he'd stand back and look at our lawn after he'd mowed it. He never looked at our lawn that way after I'd mowed it.

"WELL, WELL, WELL," said Monnie or Lucille.

On the drive home, I leaned forward and said to my father, "Was he older than you or younger?" and realized too late I should've said, "*Is* he older."

"Older," my father said.

"And how long's it been since you talked to him?"

"Long time."

"Since before I was born?"

"Uh-huh."

I didn't want to say Joanne's name, because this was after she'd bought the Thunderbird and moved out of the house, so I said, "Since before . . . *John* was born?"

"Long time."

"But why did you stop talking?"

"Just did," my father said.

My mother stared out the passenger window.

My father stared straight ahead, his eyes dark and hard as two slugs from a .22.

. . .

My eyes probably looked the same way in the waiting room of the burn unit. Al Laven went on and on about John's life, John's friendship. And when Al Laven said "buddy," you could tell that he really meant it.

It was bad enough that John was here in a burn unit, and that we hadn't talked for five years, and that I hadn't understood whatever he'd tried to say to me in the hospital bed. But thinking about Chet and my father made all of it worse, because I couldn't help but see myself as part of our miserable family tradition.

There was nothing to do in the waiting room. We just waited. The automatic doors wheezed open—it was always just another person—and closed. Each time they closed, my mother sighed.

The gravity of the place was too much to take. The faces of my mother and sisters, all pinched with the tragedy of living on. I sat in the waiting room for as long as I could—which wasn't long—and then had to get out.

I walked through the automatic doors, out into the sunlight and the dry rush of desert air. The heat was dreamlike. It passed through you as easily as a breeze through muslin, and your muscles unclenched, and your body just gave up, since to go outside was in some sense to surrender to the heat.

That surrender is what I sought. For a few steps there was no life and no death and nothing in between. My brother and I had no quarrel with each other. The gross reality of the Maricopa County Medical Center did not exist. And the very thing that had brought me to

79

Phoenix—heat, an ungodlike blast of heat—offered me a godlike respite from its aftermath.

As I walked across the parking lot, the heat went from blessedly numbing to simply hot. I couldn't wait to get in the rental car and start up the engine. I was making an escape. An escape from the burn unit. An escape from the waiting room. An escape from the heat. By the time I turned out of the parking lot, the air conditioner was already blowing cold.

I adjusted my sunglasses and set out on what would become my usual route, a big self-made labyrinth on the streets of Phoenix. As I drove, I listened to the radio. I watched the heat waves rise from the asphalt. I admired the nearby hills and smiled at tan women in halter tops. And while my brother lay dying in a burn unit, I felt terribly, guiltily, hungrily alive.

When he got drafted into the Marine Corps, my brother did his basic training near San Diego, about two hours south of Los Angeles, but in my mind it was light-years away.

Our house had changed when Joanne moved out a few months earlier: the quiet, and the pressure, which you could feel go up when John got drafted. My father's silences—really no different than usual—seemed to take on an ominous quality. Janice and June fought constantly. And although our family was smaller by two, my mother, with her oldest daughter banished from the house and her oldest son drafted into the Marine Corps, responded with a kind of homemaking frenzy. She made us pot roasts, Jell-O molds, salmon croquettes, and once we were stuffed, she cooked for Masonic dinners at the Lodge. In our refrigerator, there was always something going bad.

John sent us letters from boot camp. My mother and my sisters read John's letters, and my father read the

San Diego Tribune he brought home every day from work. I read John's letters and anything else I could get my hands on. For me, reading was like a vacation to a different life.

> *Hello everyone:*
> *I'm in San Diego now. We left L.A. at 12:00 P.M.*
> *Tuesday night and arrived here at 2:30 A.M. Weds.*
> *and I haven't been to bed yet. They have every-*
> *thing I need here and most of the things I brought*
> *are being sent back to you. My new address is*
> > *John Howard Dolan*
> > *PLT 103 C company*
> > *MCRD*
> > *San Diego, Calif. 92140*
> *I have to go now, write me soon.*
> > > *Love,*
> > > *John*

Those first letters John sent us had the Marine Corps logo in red at the top, an eagle perched on top of the world with a big anchor behind it. Under the logo it said:

UNITED STATES MARINE CORPS
"Semper Fidelis"

I loved reading anything, but I especially loved reading those letters—and the copies of *Leatherneck*, a magazine of Marine Corps life, that John got a free subscription to just for being drafted. I must have read a lot. I don't actually remember any of the books I read at home, since in our house we had only one: *The Motors Auto Repair Manual*. But I read well enough that in school I was put into the Advanced Class, which was taught by Mrs. Hannah, a young, pretty woman with a perfect nose, thin lips, and platinum blond hair done up in a bubble. I say pretty, but when I was nine I thought Mrs. Hannah was *beautiful*—but even "beautiful" doesn't quite summon the goofy exhilaration I felt in that woman's presence.

I liked school because I got to read lots of books, and I could read pretty much whatever Mrs. Hannah put in front of me. I was reading "high-school-level" texts—whatever those were—in the fourth grade. The high point of the Advanced Class, though, was when we got to write stories. Those stories meant a great deal to me. At home, out in my swing, I'd think endlessly about the story I was working on, about how I could make it better.

I was writing a story to give to John at his graduation. I sat in the backyard swing, under the shade of the avocado tree, and made up an elaborate story about my dog, Tiger, who traveled to strange places and had strange adventures—just like John would soon be doing.

Tiger (a German shepherd in my story, a half cocker spaniel and half poodle—a cockapoo—in real life) is walking along, minding his own business, when he suddenly falls into a huge pit. But this is no ordinary huge pit. In fact it's a kind of parallel reality, filled with hidden dangers, malevolent beings who are out to get him, and lots of things to jump over.

It was a hard story to get right and, determined to do just that, I was still working on it when Mrs. Hannah

83

came around to collect our stories. When she asked for mine, I explained that I was rewriting the last part.

"What?" she said, and placed her hands on her hips in the classic stance of a bully. She didn't exactly *say* it, she spat it out like a fire-breathing dragon (I must have been reading something that featured fire-breathing dragons), and all the Advanced Class turned to watch.

I didn't know how to answer. Even as a fire-breathing dragon, Mrs. Hannah was still heart-thumpingly pretty.

"You're not finished?" she said.

I said, meekly, "No." The finished story was sitting in front of me, and so was the half-finished rewrite of the last page. Mrs. Hannah and I had different notions of what "finished" meant.

"That's *it*!" she screamed. "I've had it!"

Now, from a distance of thirty years, I can see that Mrs. Hannah was probably just having a bad day, and probably talking about her own life; but at the time I was weeping for mine. Mrs. Hannah went on to say she was going to see to it that I didn't return to the Advanced Class the following year, and she kept her word.

After school that day, I walked home stubbing my sneakers and biting my lip. Joanne was gone, John was gone. My father, in his silence, was unapproachable. My mother was frantically cooking something. Janice and June were at each other's throats. If John had been at home, I could have talked to him about it, and he would have cheered me up or given me sound advice, maybe both. But he wasn't home, so I went out in the backyard with Tiger and sat in my swing, and went on with my story about a world suddenly falling from under your feet, hidden dangers, malevolent beings, and lots of things to jump over.

> *Mom, Dad, Janice, June, & J.D.:*
> *This is the first time I've really had a chance to write a letter. The first one you got was mostly dictated to us.*
> *We left L.A. at 12:00 P.M. (after waiting 17 hours) and arrived here at 2:30 A.M. Wed. morning. We got off the bus and all got haircuts. The rest of the morning and day we spent signing papers, getting clothes, and standing at attention. We went to bed at 7:30 p.m. Wed. night. The first day was the worst but sence then its been getting better. Before we leave here we will be able to shoot the M-14, swim, hike, run 10 miles with a full pack and many other things.*
> *I will be here for 8 weeks and then go to camp Pendleton for four weeks. After that they say we get to have visitors at graduation. I hope so. Well, thats about all for now. I hope everyone is well. Please write me soon.*
> > *Love,*
> > *John*

In school, in Mrs. Hannah's class, I went into an emotional and scholastic hibernation. I spent the rest of that term—and the next eight school years, in fact—blending in with the wood-patterned Formica desks, quietly doodling on my yellow Pee-Chee folders, defacing in every conceivable manner the images of those well-adjusted, all-American students who graced the covers.

Mom:

My Sgt. told us tonight Graduation is at 10:00AM Monday 7th after that we can have base liberty and we can show you around the place. Also we get to take you to chow (lunch). Its 65¢ each, but we get to show you what our food is like. I have to have a count of how many people will be there for lunch, so could you mail me the number as soon as possible. I need it by Friday or Saturday at the latest. The Graduation will be inside. You just go through the main gate and the guards will help you park and show you where to go. I talked to Jo about maybe bringing the Vette because you can drive around the base, and I like to see it again. What do you think? If Jo can't maybe Glenn & Mick could. He's a good driver. If theres no insurance on it then, don't bother about bringing it.

    I have to get this in the mail now.

    Thanks for everything.

Love, John

We were all up early on the morning of John's Marine Corps graduation. This would be the first time we'd get to visit him since he'd gotten inducted, twelve weeks before.

Our house smelled of Aqua Net and White Shoulders, and I smelled—or more likely reeked—of Old Spice. My mom had given herself a permanent the day before, and now, in her red dress and black patent leather pumps, she stood looking out the front door, humming and every once in a while patting her dark hair into place. Soon Joanne pulled up in front of the house in her white Thunderbird, parked, then got out and walked to the garage. I heard the groan of the big springs attached to the garage door, and then heard the Corvette's engine start up.

Joanne backed the Corvette onto the driveway and got out—I thought for a moment she was going to come inside—and then I heard the springs groaning as she shut the garage door.

My father sat in the La-Z-Boy reading his newspaper, no surprise, the smoke from his Chesterfield King snaking around his head. He acted as if he somehow hadn't heard the Corvette's engine, which even at idle made everything in the house vibrate like a Magic Fingers bed in a vacation motel.

At the front door, my mom gave a small wave as Joanne drove off. After the sound of the engine had faded away, she said, "Well, time to go."

Janice came into the living room wearing a short skirt and a perfectly ironed white blouse, and her hair was done up like Joanne's. Mom had told her not to do her hair like that but she'd done it anyway, and you could tell Mom was mad from the way she looked at Janice, and that Janice knew this and liked it.

June came in next, looking somewhat rumpled. She was brushing her hair and trying to straighten her sweater—Janice's sweater, actually.

Janice looked at June and started taking quick, shallow breaths. "That's . . . *mine*," she said. Then Janice sort of addressed the whole house: "SHE'S WEARING MY SWEATER!"

"Let's not start," Mom said.

"It's mine," Janice said softly.

"You can borrow something of mine," June said.

"I don't *want* to borrow anything of yours."

I started to feel sick. Though Janice didn't look like Mrs. Hannah, she reminded me of her just then.

"You can sit in front, Janice," my mom said.

Janice slowly lifted her chin until it was pointed at June's head. Then Janice stalked out of the house, and June followed, whimpering, behind her.

That's when my father said, "I'm not going."

"What?" my mother said.

"I'm not going. You go on ahead."

"Are you serious?"

"I have things to do here."

"But we haven't seen him for—"

"You go on."

My mother snatched the car keys off the buffet and said, "Well, this is just fine." She flung the screen door open. "This is just *fine*," she said, and walked out.

I felt like I was going to throw up, and my lower lip started shaking—I couldn't make it stop. I stared at my father for a few moments. He was hidden behind his newspaper, but the silence was all around him, power-ful as rays from the sun. Then I bit down on my lip, banged the screen door open, and ran out of the house.

I was sick when we started out toward San Diego: sick that Dad hadn't come with us, sick that John would feel hurt about it, and, more than anything, sick that the story I'd written for John wasn't good enough. I knew I should've gotten him something else, but I had nothing in the world that he'd need. And thinking about my story made me feel sick about school. I hadn't told anybody what had happened to me in Mrs. Hannah's Advanced Class.

Still, I was going to get to see John in a few hours, and I felt a little better when we passed Rose Hills, and a little better still when we passed Disneyland, and a lot better when I saw the ocean. The sign that said MARINE CORPS RECRUIT DEPOT, SAN DIEGO worked like a miracle cure.

We met Joanne in the parking lot and walked to the graduation area, a bunch of bleachers called the Theater. The bleachers were filling up with families just like us, except most of those families had mothers *and* fathers.

The graduation started right on time. A Lieutenant Commander Hancock gave the invocation, and a Lieutenant Colonel Blanchard gave the presentation of awards (I'm reading these names off the yellowed graduation schedule my sister Janice saved), and a First Lieutenant Favor gave the promotions, and Lieutenant Colonel Blanchard gave the graduation address, and then Lieutenant Commander Hancock finished up with the benediction. I have no memory of any of it. But I do remember the Marine Corps band started playing after that, and all the men in the audience whispered along with the music.

> *From the halls of Mon-ta-zoo-oo-ma,*
> *To the shores of Trip-oh-lee . . .*

I felt proud and teary-eyed listening to the music, but there was no time to actually cry; we were all hustling out of the bleachers toward the reception area.

A Marine in a dress uniform came toward us and I yelled out "John!" but he went past and hugged the people behind us. So many Marines were coming toward us that it looked like an invasion. And though some of them had darker or lighter skin, and some were taller or shorter, they all looked pretty much alike. When another Marine came toward us and grinned, I wasn't even sure at first it was John.

You could see he was squirming under all the hugs and kisses, and he had to use one of Mom's Kleenexes to wipe the lipstick off his face.

John was always thin, but he was even thinner after boot camp. And he was taller, too—partly because he was wearing shiny Marine Corps shoes with thick heels, and partly because he was still just a growing boy. At the time, though, John just about matched the image of him in my mind. He was tall and strong, with a shy grin, and he gave me a hug and a pat on the back, and he was a Marine, and he was my big brother, and there was nobody on the planet I would have rather seen.

John walked us around the base and showed us the obstacle course and the parade grounds, where we watched some of the newer recruits scurry by in their bright yellow Marine Corps sweatshirts as the drill sergeants barked out orders. I asked John if it was true that they fired live rounds over your head when you crawled under the barbed-wire part of the obstacle course, since Jerry Dunlap had told me this at recess the other day.

"Of course not!" Mom said.

John looked at me and grinned, and I knew this

meant that Jerry Dunlap had been right. "Shall we go to lunch?" John said.

We all went to the battalion mess hall and ate off metal trays piled high with good food. Janice told him everything that was going on at home, and June told him everything that was going on at home, and they both made it sound as if lots of things were going on at home. Joanne told him about her job at East L.A. College and her new apartment, and Mom told him about the Lodge—the latest news about the Job's Daughters and DeMolays and Masons. I couldn't think of anything to tell him that didn't include school, so I just told him that Tiger was okay, and while I was sitting there trying to come up with something else, Joanne said, "And your Corvette's running fine." Joanne pulled the keys from her purse and tossed them to John.

He caught the keys in midair, stared at them for a moment, and said, "You brought it. Wow. You brought it."

After lunch we stopped at the PX and John bought me a bright yellow sweatshirt that said UNITED STATES MARINE CORPS in red block lettering, and underneath the lettering was a Marine Corps logo; in this one, it said SEMPER FIDELIS on a banner in the eagle's beak. I put the sweatshirt on before we left the PX. I didn't care that it was way too big, and John told me I'd grow into it. I hadn't been so proud since John had given me the Remington for Christmas.

We walked out to the parking lot, where John got in the Corvette and started it up. We all stood back and watched him—this man, this Marine—revving his engine.

I was leaning forward—I must have been, because

when John looked over at me and yelled "C'mon, Jay," I was already running toward the passenger door.

John put the Corvette in gear and eased off on the clutch, and we idled around the parking lot a few times, and though we weren't going fast, it *felt* fast because the wind was blowing against our faces, and because the other Marines and their families were openly staring at us—*us*, a couple of Marines, one in a dress uniform, one in a yellow Marine Corps sweatshirt—in our fast-looking red Corvette.

We all cried a little before we said good-bye, and as I gave John one last hug I could feel the story I'd written creeping out the back pocket of my Levi's. But I didn't want to wreck this day, this moment, so I reached back and pushed it down, hard. I didn't take it out until I was home again, and then only to wad it up and toss it in one clean arc into the wastebasket.

> *Hi everybody,*
> *Well, I'm here. Its 4:00 O'clock in the after-noon (Fri.) so I guess Its about 1:00 o'clock Friday morning in the states. Theres about 15 or 16 hours difference. We left El Toro at 1:00 A.M. Wednes-day and flew to Seattle and stayed there about 45 minutes, from there we went to Tokyo but we could not leave the plane, after they re-fueled we went to Okinawa. It was pretty nice flying in a jet, but once were in the air it was just like riding in the back seat of a car. We hit some ruff weather once and it felt like I was in my car.*
> *I might be here 6 or 7 months before going to*

V.N. or I could be here for the full 13 months.
When we first got here it was about 90 degrees and
then it started raining, its kind of funny really. The
barracks here are nice.

They have three stations on the island that play
American music and a few channels on TV that
have American shows & pictures. Channel 8 is put
on by the Armed Forces, its a service station, ha ha!
It takes about four days for a letter to get to you
and about five or six for one to get back here, so
this will probably get there too late, but Happy 4th
of July any way. Well, I'll say good-by for now but
I'll write again tomorrow. Say hello to everyone
for me.

Love

John

P.S.
I found the registration for the Vette in my seabag.
I don't know how it got there, but I'll send it back
with this letter. OK?

John

That was my summer of blowing things up. From a
teenager in the neighborhood, I bought illegal skyrock-
ets, firecrackers, cherry bombs, M-80s—even M-120s,
which were said to be equivalent to a quarter stick of
dynamite. And I played.

For the big stuff, I'd ride my bike up to McCaslin's
Pit, a gravel yard not far from our house. I'd blow up
cans, boxes, mounds of dirt—anything. Once I found a
carcass of a snake, which I blew up.

At home, under the avocado tree in the backyard,

I'd dig miniature trenches and people them with green plastic soldiers. Sometimes I'd camouflage the trenches with twigs and leaves, elaborate patterns meant to hide the life underneath. And then I'd blow them up.

One day, I tagged along with my father when he went to work: his Greyhound route from Los Angeles to San Diego and back. My father was up every morning at 4:00. He'd have breakfast and leave the house at 4:45. He'd be at the bus station downtown by 5:15 and boarding his passengers by 5:45 sharp. I found all of this out by riding to work with him that day, having slept through all the other mornings of his work routine.

I sat just across the aisle from the driver's seat, and on the way to San Diego I saw my father flash his headlights in the early morning light, and at one of the houses alongside the freeway, I saw a man warming up his car in his driveway. The man flashed his headlights in return.

"Who's that?" I said.

"I don't know," my father said.

"Then why'd you flash your lights at him?"

"I see him every day," he said.

My father drove on. The sun was coming up, blue sky, glimpses of ocean, the traffic getting thicker on Highway 5. Most of the other passengers were asleep.

"You don't know his name?" I said.

"Nope, never met him."

"Well, how long have you been doing that?"

My father shrugged. "Years," he said.

· · ·

94

When we passed Camp Pendleton, I asked my father if he'd ever stopped and said hello to John.

Still keeping the bus perfectly aligned between the white lines, my father turned and looked at me as if I was a creature from another planet. "Of course not!" he said.

That Christmas, John called home from Okinawa—a big event. He'd written and told us exactly what time he'd call, and we all sat staring at the telephone as our father's new GREYHOUND 20 YEARS OF SAFE DRIVING clock on the buffet chimed five o'clock.

John had sent us a big box a week earlier, and in it were our Christmas presents. There was a tiny Minolta spy camera for Janice, a Sony radio for June, a reel-to-reel tape recorder for Joanne. There was a hand-embroidered tablecloth for my mother and a set of miniature Masonic tools made of ivory for my father. And I got a pair of binoculars in a leather case, a samurai-sword letter opener, and a pocketknife with a green butterfly handle and a stainless steel blade.

There was something of a scramble when the telephone rang, but our father, who seldom spoke on the phone or otherwise, got up from the La-Z-Boy and said, "I'll get it."

Dad cleared his throat and picked up the phone. He said, "Hello. Yes, operator, I accept. Hello!" He waited for a moment, then said, "Hel—uh . . . fine, fine. Everything okay over there?" He nodded. "Need anything?" he said, by which he meant money. He was already leaning toward Mom with the receiver; it was as if the receiver was hot and if he kept at it much longer his ear would get burned. "Well," he said, "if you need anything, let us know," and by "us" he meant Mom. Then he said, "Okay, merry Christmas, here's your mother."

After Mom, I got to go next.

"Hi, John," I said. There was a lag of a few seconds while our voices passed each other somewhere mid-Pacific, but when I didn't hear an immediate reply I got worried and said, "Are you okay?"

"Hi, Jay," he said.

"Thanks for the neat stuff," I said.

"I'm fine," he said.

"So what's it like in Okinawa?"

"Yeah, I thought you'd like that."

"What?" I said. "What's it like over there?"

"How's school?" John said.

I still felt sick at the mention of school—and would for years—but my whole family was standing there watching me. "Fine," I said.

"It's pretty," he said.

"What?" I said.

"Listen," he said, "you have a merry Christmas, Jay, and I'll see you real soon."

My eyes were getting watery, and I wiped at them with the sleeve of my faded yellow Marine Corps sweatshirt, and I said in the same voice I would use twenty years later, at John's bedside in a burn unit in Phoenix, "John . . . John . . ." as the receiver was gently pulled from my hand.

Sometimes I'd be halfway across town when it struck me I needed to get back—*now*—and then Phoenix became a kind of racecourse. Stop signs meant slow, yellow lights meant green, and green lights meant no light at all. The rental car leaned heavily in turns, and sometimes I managed power slides on the sandy asphalt. I imagined getting pulled over by the police and telling them that my brother was in the burn unit at Maricopa County Medical Center. What better earthly reason to drive so fast?

But I never got pulled over, and the main response I got was a raised middle finger from some rightfully annoyed driver—soon just a blip in my rearview mirror.

I felt a chill whenever I walked back into the burn unit. It was cold in the waiting room, and almost everywhere else in Phoenix. My mother and three sisters turned and looked up as I walked through the automatic doors, and though they smiled, I could see they were disappointed that it was just me.

"They took John into debriding," Janice said.

Debriding (it's pronounced de-*breeding*) is, I found out, where the dead or dying skin is surgically removed. His wounds—90 percent of his skin—were becoming septic. The skin is removed with a scalpel that one of the nurses, years later, would describe as "a whacker." After this, John's body would be stapled with pigskin or cadaver skin, until his healthy skin (that 10 percent) could be "harvested"—that is, surgically removed, stretched, and moved to another part of his body. The hospital's Death Summary reads, "As much debridement was performed as could be tolerated by the patient in his condition."

It did not seem possible that my brother could have been in such a catastrophe and then have to go through this. It did not seem possible that things could get any worse.

Things got worse. On my second day in Phoenix, John's kidneys failed. He'd been in the hospital for six days. The doctors explained that his kidneys simply couldn't handle the massive infection, and that the next step was to put John on dialysis.

There was always a next step. Fluid lines, respirators, catheters, debriding, massive amounts of drugs.

All of this was explained clearly and logically, and yet what had happened in the explosion, what had caused all this, was neither clear nor logical; it was, in most respects, unimaginable.

The Mohave Generating Station is a massive coal-fired, superheated-steam power plant, with a boiler about nine stories high. Its twin turbines have a combined rating of 1,580 megawatts—about 5 percent of Southern California Edison's entire output. Not too long ago, I asked one of the survivors of the explosion just how much electricity that was. He thought for a moment and said, "It could light up all of Las Vegas." Then he nodded and said, "Easy."

The Public Utilities Commission's Executive Summary would, in 1991, describe the explosion this way:

> On June 9, 1985, a thirty inch seam welded pipe on the reheat section of the Mohave Generating Station Unit 2 burst open without warning. The steam was oriented toward the control building. The steam line contained 1000°F steam at approximately 618 psig. This steam was released directly toward the north wall of the control room. It broke through a temporary plywood wall and filled the control room with steam and asbestos from the insulation that covered the steam line.

In the waiting room, when I asked him again to explain what had happened, Al Laven was more succinct. "It's at really high temperature and really high pressure."

"What's 'really'?" I said.

Al thought for a minute and said, "Well, it's so hot that the steam, past a certain point, isn't even steam. We call it 'stuff.' And when there's a pinhole leak up on one of the pipes, when we go up there, we tie a rag on the end of an old broom handle and hold it in front of us. If we see the rag get cut in half, we stop."

"It'll cut a rag in half?" I said.

"It'll cut a body in half," he said.

I went into the burn unit, to John's bedside, every few hours. We took turns, and if I could, I avoided taking mine when Janice and June were in the room. Janice was frighteningly upbeat about every procedure the doctors took. "YOU'RE GONNA GET WELL!" she'd scream at our brother's inert and ravaged body, a body that bore no resemblance to the man, much less the boy, I once knew. His skin was changing from bright red to bright yellow— it was puffy and tight—and there were fine crosshatched lines on his knees and elbows that looked like the grill marks on a steak. The doctors made those cuts so the swollen skin wouldn't split.

Janice seemed to believe that through sheer will— her will—John would survive. Our father's death, ten months earlier, had hit Janice harder than any of us— including, I think, our mother. Now Janice was faced with losing her older brother, and she simply wouldn't tolerate any pessimistic thoughts, of which I had many.

"What kind of life could he live?" I said in the waiting room, not really asking but wondering aloud.

My mother took a deep breath and sighed. She'd held up remarkably well after my father died; he'd been ill for so long that his death seemed—especially for her, to everyone but Janice—a blessing. Mom seemed resigned that John was going to die, although she didn't rule out a miracle and accepted the doctors' efforts as necessary and good. Back at the hotel, away from Janice, Mom said, "I was raised on a farm. I've seen a lot of animals die. I can see it in John's eyes. He's dying."

In the waiting room, Janice said, "They're debriding him now. That's good. They're going to get rid of the bad skin so the good skin can grow back."

Bad skin? That was John, that was our brother's flesh, and he was being flayed alive.

"YOU'RE LOOKING BETTER," Janice would scream when they wheeled John's bloated, comatose body back into his room, his once-strong arms now bandaged and suddenly as thin as a young boy's.

June, though less loud than Janice, also seemed to hear only part of the doctors' updates—the reasons John would benefit from the procedure. "He's already starting to look better," she'd say back in the waiting room, and I'd stare at her.

"He is," she'd say. "I know he is."

When I reminded June what the doctors had said—that they probably would have to amputate his fingers, and possibly his hands—she said, "But they're not sure yet. There's always a miracle."

Janice eyed June. Her chewing gum snapped. She twirled a strand of hair. This was Janice's sentiment exactly, but she wouldn't go so far as to agree completely with June, even on matters of life and death.

"They discover new cures every day," Janice said—at once an agreement, a rebuttal, and a correction. During the many years of our father's illness, Janice had steadfastly refused to believe that he would die, and with his many recoveries, she was often right. For Janice, being right was more important than being truthful.

"It's probably too early to tell yet," said Joanne. "We'll just have to wait and see."

Janice and June and I nodded, as if Joanne had just agreed, exactly, with each of us.

At times it did seem as if this catastrophe had reduced us to ourselves, as if we really did live inside the petty roles of childhood—Joanne the big sister, the peacemaker; Janice the middle child, with a middle child's resentment; June the youngest girl, her naïveté transformed into disappointment; and me the baby, who would rather be done with it quickly, then go outside and play—or, in this case, drive.

Sitting there with us, but often very much by herself, was our mother. She, too, had been reduced to herself. She had lost cousins, uncles, aunts; she had lost parents and grandparents; she had lost brothers and sisters and close friends. She had lost her husband of forty years less than a year ago. And now she was losing a child.

She sighed deeply, her shoulders rounded with the weight of loss.

We were, the rest of us, losing a brother—but he was more than that. John was not the same brother, the same person, the same hero to each of us. Because in losing our brother we were losing a part of ourselves, but for each of us it was a different part.

After a long day at the burn unit, we'd finally go back to the hotel, where, harried and numb and exhausted, we did things like shower and sleep. Joanne and Janice shared a suite, my mother and I shared one, and June had one to herself. Sometimes we went out for dinner first, since what we'd eaten during the day was hospital cafeteria food and vending machine swill. These dinners were often as tasteless as the food that we'd snatched during the day, because if we talked about John we couldn't eat, and it felt wrong to talk about anything else.

One night, after just such a dinner, I went down to the front desk and checked for messages—by which I mean a message from the *Mississippi Review*. I'd called the magazine's managing editor and asked her to let me know as soon as she had copies of the *Mississippi Review* number 39, the issue my story was in.

The act of stopping at a hotel's front desk and checking for messages was something I'd done so many times during my years on the road that I could feel my-self assuming an old familiar posture of self-importance and purpose: a kind of brutal efficiency, a quick flick of the wrist to check the time, a man with places to go, people to—et cetera. I didn't like this posture, didn't want to be that man anymore, and yet there was some comfort in it. Maybe, I figured (as I stared gravely at my watch face), the *Mississippi Review* would change all of that.

The desk clerk was kind enough to check for my messages, even though he probably knew that every message had already been delivered, and then told me, no, sorry, no messages yet, and asked if I wanted a wake-up call. This man was thin, with reddish-blond hair, and his voice had a slightly effeminate ring to it. He wrote down the information and wished me a good night, and I thanked him and headed back to my suite.

My mother had already closed the door to her room, but I could still hear the mumbled breaths of her troubled sleep. I looked around my room feeling whipped. I usually tried to time it so there was no gap between falling into bed and falling asleep, but this night it seemed impossible—and sleep itself a great effort—so I set out for the hotel bar for a drink.

I sat at the bar and sipped at a single-malt scotch and wrote in my journal, *I can't believe this is happening.* I couldn't have invented a story like this—a guy who's pissed off at the world for years, a guy who's burning up inside, fetches up in a burn unit in *Phoenix*, of all places. The older brother doesn't talk, and the younger brother chooses words as his vocation. The older brother, the dying brother, is thirty-nine, and very soon the younger brother will be holding his first publication, the proof of his new life, the thirty-ninth issue of the *Mississippi Review*. I shook my head at the thought of Joanne's Thunderbird—another name for a phoenix, which as everybody knows is a bird that rises from the ashes of a fire. Who would believe such coincidences? Who would believe such a story?

I noticed the cocktail waitress looking at me, and when I lifted my glass of scotch and tried to smile, my face felt like it was splitting open.

As I lay in bed that night, I kept thinking about the desk clerk; there was something unsettling about him, and I couldn't figure out what it was. Then I remembered Richard Cannon.

When I was growing up, Richard lived across the street from us. He was the same age as John, and they were best friends. Richard was thin, with reddish-blond hair and a slightly whiny voice, and he was sensitive and smart and had good taste, and in high school he became interested in architecture and interior design.

People used to size him up pretty quickly. Once, when one of my father's friends was visiting, my mother pointed out the window and said, "And that's Richard Cannon. He likes art." My father's friend glanced out the window and said, "Art who?"

In high school, of course, he was branded a sissy by John's other friends, and if Richard was a sissy, then what did that make John—his boyfriend? Such was the teen dilemma John found himself in.

My brother must have struggled with this for a while, but finally the pressure was just too much, and he dumped the friendship.

Once John made this decision, it was as if Richard Cannon didn't exist, which was quite a feat, considering that he went to the same school and lived right across the street. John never gave Richard any explanation, simply told him that he wasn't going to give him a ride to school anymore, and never said anything to him ever again—even decades later, when both of them happened to be visiting their parents at Christmas. Richard Cannon, arriving with his wife and kids, would sometimes look hesitantly at John. And John would get out of his car without acknowledging Richard's presence, then walk steel-jawed into our parents' house to celebrate peace on earth and goodwill to men.

The mornings in the desert were beautiful. The air was dry and cool—a comforting coolness, as it carried the promise of warmth. The hotel had a courtyard with a kidney-shaped pool filled with bright blue water, and on some mornings I'd get up early and stroll out to the pool and dive into water so close in temperature to the air that it seemed as if I was diving not into water but into blue.

Then I'd get out and, still damp, go for a drive before breakfast. I drove with no destination in mind. The idea wasn't to get anywhere but to settle into a rhythm, to find new ways of moving through the desert. I'd drive down one street for a few miles, then turn, drive a few more miles, and though I never really learned the streets of Phoenix, I always ended up back in the same place— the Maricopa County Medical Center. The hotel was close to the hospital and easy to find, but I knew how to get to it only from the hospital. The hospital was always the beginning and the end. I'd slow down, look, then drive on. I'd turn the radio up and listen to the oldies station playing my past—Ricky Nelson crooning "I'm a travelin' man . . ." and Elvis Presley belting out "Viva Las Vegas"—as I drove through my life, my family's lives, our lives together.

When I came back from these drives, I'd usually find my mother sitting by herself at one of the small tables out in the courtyard, with her daily breakfast of toast, coffee, and a small bowl of fruit. After growing up on a farm during the Depression, she never seemed certain there would be enough food. Even now, she can't stand the taste of milk or chicken, from her chores of early morning milkings and midmorning neck-wringings. And she gets queasy at the sight of a body of water, from when one of her brothers threw her into an irrigation ditch and "taught" her to swim.

The hotel's complimentary breakfast buffet, not far from our table, would be arrayed with chafing dishes heaped with bacon, scrambled eggs, sausages, toast, and French toast; there were baskets of muffins and Danishes and croissants; pitchers of chilled orange juice, apple juice, tomato juice; big pots filled with steaming coffee; plates of halved cantaloupes and huge bowls brimming with neatly trimmed fruit.

My mother would invariably smile and ask if I'd had a good drive, then ask if I wanted some of her toast.

We wore different faces in the morning. First thing, it was possible to enjoy sitting outside at a table half in sunlight, half in shade; it was possible to enjoy a cup of coffee, and to talk to each other about nothing, nothing at all.

Then Janice would come down to breakfast. She had an edgy impatience with my mother, and my mother reciprocated.

"Good morning," Janice would say, as if issuing a challenge.

"Good morning," my mother would say, without the musical inflection those two words had when she said them to the rest of us.

It had always been like this. When Janice was eighteen months old, my mother gave birth to June, and my father, necessarily, took care of Janice. She'd always remained close to our father, her ally, and our mother was her enemy. So Janice loved our father first, then Joanne and John. She sometimes tolerated June, now. Me, the youngest, she ignored or held in contempt.

It was hard for me to believe that whatever difficulties existed between my mother and Janice were not Janice's fault, even though my mother—then white-haired and seventy—sometimes behaved like a wolverine if it meant giving up an inch in their dealings.

Once, when I was little, Janice walked by the bathroom while I was pissing. I'd left the door open a little, and Janice looked in and watched me aiming the stream of piss at the bubbles on the surface of the water—a game that I'd played and never particularly thought about.

"What are you doing?" she said.

"Nothing," I said, suddenly embarrassed.

Janice came into the bathroom, then told me that I should tell her what I'd been doing because she was my friend, and that I could trust her because she was my friend, and that if I didn't trust her she wouldn't be my friend, and I wanted her to be my friend, didn't I?

She made me promise to show her my game, and the next time I went to the bathroom, I dutifully fetched Janice and showed her how I pissed in the toilet.

Later that afternoon, I walked into the living room to held-back laughter—my mother, my aunt Leota, Joanne—and Janice telling them precisely how I pissed, and then asking me to show them.

The kind of loathing and distrust I felt for Janice that day was roughly the same twenty-five years later, when she simply came down to breakfast at the hotel, or when, at the hospital, she screamed at John's swollen, ravaged body, "YOU'RE LOOKING BETTER!"

When John was a Marine in Okinawa, Janice was a teenager in Monterey Park. Joanne had moved out, John had shipped out, and Janice was suddenly the oldest and ready to prove it.

One of John's friends, Jack Ottie (yet another friend who didn't get drafted), had a brother named Joe (presumably undrafted too), and Joe asked Janice out.

My mother interceded, said absolutely not. Janice went into the kind of rage that until then she'd saved for June. She screamed at my mother, "You're just jealous—you've always been jealous!" and my mother screamed back, "You're rotten—and you've always been rotten!"

Janice wrote John about the injustice she'd suffered, and John wrote back that Mom's judgment of Joe Ottie's character was probably right, then seconded her opinion by saying, "Besides that, he drives a Volvo."

By the time John came home from Okinawa, Janice was dating anybody she wanted, and she always seemed to want to date older men. One of the first, Steve Wasden, had been a semiprofessional motorcycle racer. He told us stories of his motorcycle races—mostly flat-track—and John and I listened with great interest, my father with skepticism and interest. Janice seemed interested that we found him interesting. She never seemed to care very much for Steve, although he seemed to adore her. She twirled a lock of her hair and watched him, and watched us watching him.

Steve Wasden gave me one of his motorcycle trophies (second place), probably to prove his credentials to my doubting father. He also gave me an old Honda 55 so I could say I owned a motorcycle—and probably to impress my sister.

A Honda 55 looks more like a motor *scooter* than a motor*cycle*. The engine's dinky, the gas tank is under the seat, and its frame is open, like a girl's bicycle. In old movies set in Third World countries, you see lots of Honda 55s like the one Steve Wasden gave me, the only difference being that those Honda 55s actually ran. Mine was a flat-tired, broken-mufflered, rusty piece of shit. It didn't run, it hadn't run in years, and Steve Wasden comforted my mother with the assurance that it probably never would run.

My brother got the Honda 55 running. He rebuilt the carburetor, changed the oil and the spark plug, cleaned the rust from the engine—which wasn't as bad as it looked. He took off the lights and gutted all but the essentials of the electrical system. He took off the flat tires and put on knobbies, and put a sixty-tooth sprocket on the back.

I had no idea what a "sprocket" was, or what it was supposed to do, but I loved the word; and I bragged to my friends that not only did I have a motorcycle, I had one with a sixty-tooth sprocket.

What this particular sprocket did, I discovered, was make the gearing of my motorcycle—and thus the speed—incredibly low. My Honda 55 could only go about thirty-five miles an hour, but it could, with a spindly kid on it, churn through or over just about anything—sand or mud, hills or desert. My brother transformed my Third World motor scooter into a passable off-road dirt bike.

Then John bought a motorcycle for himself, a new white Yamaha 125 Enduro—a *real* off-road machine! Each weekend, we'd load the motorcycles into an old blue trailer and tow it with our parents' Oldsmobile out to the desert. My brother wore his old Marine Corps fatigues and combat boots, and I wore blue jeans and my faded yellow Marine Corps sweatshirt, its sleeves long ago cut off. It was just the two of us out there riding the trails, John usually going slow enough for me to keep up. If he rode on ahead, he always circled back to see if I was okay; when he did, I'd wave at him or pop a wheelie, and he'd wave or pop a wheelie back. Such was our conversation, and it was enough. Just then—for a little while—I might've been the little brother John had always wanted.

Steve Wasden noticed our enthusiasm and offered to take us out to the desert races. One Saturday morning, we followed him out into the desert. He didn't tow some old trailer behind an Oldsmobile—he drove a custom Ford van. And he didn't ride a Honda 55 or even a new Yamaha 125 Enduro—he rode a racing bike, a sleek, loud 250 Bultaco. Every now and then, as we drove down the highway, we'd see a slash of chalk from a bag that had been thrown onto the shoulder of the road. Those slashes were our signposts. When we saw three slashes of chalk, we'd reached the turnoff into what might as well have been a secret world. Everything was suddenly dust, in which there were trucks and vans behind us, trucks and vans in front of us. Desert racers.

Steve somehow led us through the miasma to the campsite of the Invaders Motorcycle Club—a club whose name and hot-pink logo came from an eponymous science fiction TV series. In *The Invaders,* visitors from another planet tried each week to destroy the earth. These aliens were visible to only one human being, who managed every seven days to save the earth from destruction. I never really understood the connection between the TV show and the motorcycle club, but it didn't matter. The Invaders had a cool logo, a lot of friendly people, and—very soon—a new member named John Dolan.

Every Friday night, as soon as John got off work, we'd drive out to the races. That is, John drove and I slept. He'd bought an old Ford Econoline van, in which he loaded all our gear: the motorcycles, the helmets, the ice chest and the tool kit, the gas cans, the two-by-eight board we used as a ramp, and the sleeping bags and blankets I usually burrowed into as soon as the drive started. I slept between the motorcycles, and below the web of ropes that held them securely upright.

Sometimes I'd feel the van gently veer to one side—I knew—to avoid a suicidal jackrabbit. These were big jackrabbits; they'd leap onto the highway, stop, then look at you with startled red eyes. My brother and I knew the rules of the road like a catechism—true sons of Greyhound—and the relevant rule here was: *Never avoid hitting an animal if it risks killing the people in your vehicle.* Sleeping, I'd feel my brother let up on the gas for a moment, feel the gentle swerve, and sometimes, from my sleep, I could even *see* the jackrabbit just before I heard the *whump* beneath me. Then I felt my brother easing the van back into its lane and resuming speed. But the motorcycles never shifted. My brother was expert at knot tying.

On Sunday mornings, I'd wake up in the desert—in some sense our church. Always a few others were already awake, sitting near a campfire and drinking coffee. I'd go over to warm up, and they'd give me a cup of hot chocolate, and I'd listen to their stories: of crashing in a cactus patch, of finding the ground suddenly missing beneath them, like something from a cartoon; of thinking they were doing great in a race, only to be lapped by J.N. Roberts—and a desert race had only two laps, and each one was fifty miles.

The Invaders had several expert riders (Randy Milligan was at one time sixth in the 100 cc expert division), but most were in the amateur division, or, like my brother, in the novice division. But the Invaders' most famous rider was John McGowan, who raced with his dog, Kooky, standing on his gas tank.

In the documentary film *On Any Sunday,* there's a scene with John McGowan and Kooky coming into the pits. They hop off their Husqvarna 400 and gulp some water—Kooky from a bowl, McGowan from a bottle—while the pit crew fills their gas tank. Then Kooky pisses on a sagebrush. Then both of them hop back on the motorcycle—Kooky standing on his carpeted patch on the gas tank—and ride off into the desert. In that scene, I'm the spindly kid in the background.

I spent a lot of time in the background at those races. I rode my Honda 55 between the Invaders' camp and the pits, or sometimes out to the last check-point to watch the racers come through. In the three years that John and I went, the racer who came through first nearly every time was J.N. Roberts—the number one desert racer in the country. He was so good that Rich Thorwaldson—at number two—switched from desert races to motocross. Unless his Husqvarna 400 broke down, which wasn't often, J.N. Roberts would win, and sometimes he won even with a breakdown.

On Saturdays, my brother and I rode together. We'd ride out through sand washes, or over the sagebrush-high ridges called whoop-de-doos, or else we would hang out in camp. At night, we sat around campfires, and the Invaders drank beer and told stories and laughed. There were campfires all around us—dozens of clubs, hundreds and sometimes thousands of racers. Not one of those racers would leave you stranded in the desert. If you broke down on the course, somebody from your club would come help you. If your van broke down on the road, *anybody* who drove by would help you. And in that sense we were a family, if what you expect from family is loyalty and kindness, good humor, and a certain largeness of heart.

In the waiting room, we waited. Janice and Mom didn't argue. They were civil to each other, but even in the midst of this tragedy, there was still the tension of a lifetime between them.

"Do you want some coffee, Mother?" Janice said. She was the only one who called our mother "Mother." The rest of us called her "Mom."

"Yes," Mom said.

"Here."

"Thank you."

Al Laven was back from the burn unit in Las Vegas. He'd driven there to see some of the other victims, then to Laughlin for a funeral, the first of six that resulted from the explosion. John's funeral, a few weeks later, would be the last.

Al was upbeat and diligent. He kept us informed of everything, acted as our liaison with Southern

California Edison, reminded us again and again of John's many great qualities, and steadfastly refused to believe he wasn't going to pull through.

Janice nodded vigorously at Al Laven's goodwill, and when I questioned it, when I asked, with all of his suffering, what kind of life could John live, Janice turned a cold shoulder to me, literally: she pulled the shoulder of her sweater up and turned toward Al Laven. "Go on," she said.

We couldn't all go into the burn unit at once, but two or three of us could go in at a time, and if it was at all possible, I went in without Janice. Sometimes I lingered at the sink near the entrance, soaping my hands slowly, and slowly putting on my baby blue paper shoe covers, my gown, my cap, my surgeon's mask.

I could hear Janice at the other end of the burn unit, in John's room. "YOU'RE LOOKING GOOD, JOHN. YOU'RE GETTING STRONGER." When Janice was screaming this way, I saw, more than once, a doctor close the door to his office.

June was equally insistent, though not quite as loud. "WE LOVE YOU, JOHNNY. YOU'RE GONNA GET WELL."

They behaved like a cheerleading section shouting down Death—and I hated them for that. John was dying; death was the only thing he had left, but they wouldn't allow him to die with any dignity. Just then, I hated them both. I hated their self-righteous spectacle, the loudness and shamelessness of their lies. They were lying to the one person in my life who'd never lied to me. But what I hated most was that their love for my brother was blinding and unbounded; they didn't give a good goddamn if they made a spectacle, and wouldn't consider John's nightmarish future, only what was in front of them: their big brother, whom they desperately wanted to live.

I wish I could've felt the same.

As they made their way out of John's room, I made my way in. When we passed in the doorway, we looked at one another, and though we all wore our surgeon's masks, we each knew what was hidden underneath.

I went with hesitation into John's room, still afraid my presence might make him rise shaking from his bed, his eyes two pinpoints of anger. I was flattering myself. The man was dying; my presence was irrelevant. I stood quietly beside his body for a while before I spoke—not from any sense of propriety but because I didn't know what to say. And in all likelihood he couldn't hear me, couldn't hear even Janice's cheerleading, through the sea of drugs in which he was swimming. The heart monitor beside his bed was wired to his chest like a timing light, and the blips on its screen offered proof that Janice's and June's visits had exactly the same effect as mine—which is to say, none.

Sometimes, though, there was a flicker of muscle, a shudder of life that had nothing to do with me, and I'd lean close and say softly, "John, it's Jay. I'm here with you. It's Jay. I'm here with you."

At those moments, I too wanted to believe that my brother was going to make it. I thought of his good luck in the Marine Corps, and of his dogged determination when we rode motorcycles out in the desert.

The starting line of a race was sometimes a mile wide, with hundreds or thousands of racers anxious to tear off into the desert, out toward the smoke bomb—a huge pile of old tires soaked with diesel and then set ablaze. By the time J.N. Roberts reached the smoke bomb, dozens of other racers had already broken down, crashed, or quit.

The rest of the riders had to contend with what J.N. did not: dust. The only time he ever rode through dust was when he started lapping people. So, for the others, there were rocks, dust, traffic, dust, heat, confusion, dust, drop-offs, mine shafts, dust, and now and then a cactus patch. A desert race was a lot like a marathon, in both exertion and time: the elite finished in about two hours; the rest, those lucky enough to even finish, straggled in throughout the afternoon and sometimes into the evening.

To finish a desert race was no small achievement, and my brother, more often than not, was a finisher. When he came into the pits, I was his pit crew. I'd have a jug of iced water all ready, along with a towel to wipe the dust off his goggles and his face, and the gas can with his number painted on the side. My preparation helped, but there was really no need to shave precious seconds from his pit stop. He often shut his engine off, walked over to the van, and, deeply exhausted, sat down for a few minutes on an ice chest. He'd just ridden through fifty miles of virgin desert and dust, and had another fifty miles of the same ahead of him—then he had to load up our motorcycles and drive for three hours to get us home.

Once, as he sat resting in the pits after his first lap, J.N. Roberts came by after his *second* lap; he was about to win the race, and win it easily. Somebody pointed a movie camera at J.N. as he rode by, and J.N. saw the man with the camera and waved just as his Husqvarna 400 began to slide into a turn. J.N. gave the throttle a little more gas to *increase* the slide. His feet never left the pegs, and his motorcycle slid in perfect control, and he waved as easily as a man sitting in a beach chair—all just for the fun of it, and for a few seconds in some-body's home movie.

"Wow," I said.

John nodded, smiled. Then he got up and walked stiffly toward his motorcycle, ready to get back into a race that somebody else had already won.

I thought about that as John lay in his hospital bed with respirator tubes in his nose, IVs in his arms, a dry catheter running from his groin, and with skin so red and swollen that his face was barely recognizable.

I wanted to believe it. There were moments when I really *did* believe it: *This is not the end. It is not over yet. My brother is a finisher . . .*

As I was growing up, I didn't get many of my brother's or sisters' hand-me-down toys or clothes, since nobody in my family had ever imagined there would be another kid to hand anything down to. My sister June, the closest to me in age, was seven years older. In our backyard, I'd swing in the old rusted swing set, or sometimes I'd wander over into the playhouse that my father had built when my brother and sisters were little. My sisters remember playing in a playhouse, its roof shingled, its walls painted white, its windows with glass panes and gingham curtains. I remember playing in the ruins of a playhouse, its wood long stripped of paint, its fallen shingles a flying *whang* in my face whenever the lawn mower happened to kick one of them up, its windows square holes in the walls, and the walls themselves in various angles of collapse until the day I took my father's claw hammer from its place in the garage and tore the thing down.

My Honda 55, a hand-me-down of sorts, made up for all of that.

I truly loved that little piece of shit. When Steve Wasden brought it over, I was delirious with excitement, but also disappointed at the sight of its broken muffler, its red paint faded to the color of a bruise, its rusted wheels and flat tires, its gas tank *under* the seat.

"That gives it better weight distribution at high speed," Steve said, and laughed, then John laughed. I laughed, too, but secretly started to believe it.

For two years I rode that Honda 55 with all my heart through sand washes and mud bogs, fields of bottlebrush and sage, and up hills with dizzying in-clines—and this last I loved the best. Many runners could probably beat my top speed. But with its famous sprocket and its knobby tires, my Honda 55 could churn slowly up steep hills that more powerful motorcycles often could not, because the riders weren't used to going so slow, applied too much power, lost traction, and spun out.

They often smiled condescendingly at my Honda 55 at the bottom of such a hill. I'd watch them rev up and spin dust as they attacked the hill, only to lose momen-tum and purchase halfway up. That's when I started up the hill at a crawl, with all the power of a sewing machine, inching my way up and always turning my head to repay a condescending smile to the spun-out rid-ers as I rode past.

Still, we didn't do many hill climbs. We rode mostly in the great, wide-open Mojave, where if the riders paused long enough to look at me as they flew by, they laughed.

. . .

One day in November, after a year and a half on his Yamaha 125 Enduro, my brother bought not just a new off-road motorcycle but a *racing* motorcycle, and not just any racing motorcycle but *the* racing motorcycle: a Husqvarna 250, the same make that J. N. Roberts rode, albeit with a slightly smaller engine.

It was a wonderful machine—all power and efficiency, with no lights and not even a kickstand, because a Husqvarna 250 was not built for standing still. Even its seat was uncomfortable, because the right way to ride a Husqvarna 250 was to stand on the pegs, clamp the gas wide open, then hang on as you flew across the desert in perfect control, with the Husqvarna bucking underneath you and sometimes high enough that the uncomfortable seat would smack you gently in the butt. Its engine had huge cooling fins, and its gas tank was bright red with an oval of chrome on each side, and it was beautiful, and it was my brother's, and I was proud of it, and of him.

When we went out to the races now, my brother didn't so much stand out as blend in—everybody had fast, exotic motorcycles. Almost everybody. I still had my Honda 55. But while my brother had the Yamaha up for sale, it was mine to ride. What a joy it was to roll those motorcycles out of the van in the Invaders' camp! What a joy to see John on his Husqvarna, and to see myself on the Yamaha. And I could see myself in the way people looked at me: no condescending smiles, no laughter, just a serious glance to size up another desert racer, one of their own tribe. It wasn't going to last long, I knew, but I enjoyed it anyway.

For Christmas that year, I was angling for a new pair of gloves—leather racing gloves, expensive ones, with extra padding in the palms and strips of hard rubber sewn onto the tops of the fingers to protect your hands when you hit sagebrush at high speed. For me to want such gloves was comical, since my Honda 55 didn't *have* a high speed. But when you walked around in the pits, who knew? I often ditched the bike by the van and walked around the pits, and for this I definitely needed a pair of leather high-speed racing gloves.

I got a pair of gloves that Christmas. They were plain brown workman's gloves, from my mother. I knew she'd talked to John, and that John had told her about the gloves, and that in the translation something—everything—had been lost. There were the usual gifts: a nice shirt from Joanne, some Pee-Chee folders from Janice, a tiny transistor radio from June, some J. C. Penney underwear from Santa, and only an envelope from John. Inside was a card that read MERRY CHRISTMAS, LOVE, JOHN. And Scotch-taped to the card was a key with a Yamaha logo.

I walked out to the garage and stared at my shiny, near-new Yamaha 125 Enduro—a motor*cycle*! I sat on the seat, and though I'd ridden it quite a bit, the motorcycle felt different, and I felt different on it. I put the key in the ignition, turned it. I could hear the gasoline sloshing in the gas tank. I reached down to turn on the gas, and in the handlebars' spotless chrome I could see my happy, distorted reflection. Then I stood high on the pegs and stomped on the kick starter and the Yamaha's engine growled to life, and its racing pipe, unmuffled, high-pitched and loud, announced my very merry Christmas to the whole neighborhood.

When I saw John later that day and thanked him, he just smiled and said, "Be careful."

I was transformed by that motorcycle. At school—in the seventh grade, by then—I was able to endure five mind-numbing days a week because come Saturday morning I knew where I'd be.

Out on the desert, I rode my Yamaha around the pits with the twitching self-consciousness of a boy whose voice was changing—which mine, coincidentally, was. The motorcycle was really a little too powerful and heavy for a still-spindly kid, so I continued to ride between the Invaders' camp and the pits, or out to the last checkpoint, but I knew that soon I'd be a desert racer, and a great one—like J.N. Roberts.

One of the last races we went to was also one of the biggest ever. Most usually had anywhere from five hundred to a thousand riders; this one had over two thousand. With the binoculars John had sent me from Okinawa strapped around my neck, I rode my Yamaha 125 just past the last checkpoint and waited for the racers to come through. I'd found a perfect spot: a high hill that overlooked a dry lake that the racers' motorcycles would soon be screaming across. But it was perfect for another reason, too: the lake bed was crossed by a deep gully. Expert racers would drop into it, then go airborne as they came up the other side; amateurs would have a little more trouble, since the slopes on either side of the gully would soon be covered with deep, loose dirt; and novices would ride into not a gully as much as a tractionless dust bowl, where they would get stuck, or crash, or both.

My brother did both.

But first through, as always, was J.N. Roberts. I watched through the binoculars as a plume of dust came across the dry lake at—I'm guessing—seventy or eighty miles an hour. But J.N. evidently didn't see what was suddenly in front of him. He didn't let off on the gas, and he and his motorcycle flew across the gully like an airplane at takeoff. He nearly cleared it, but his back tire hit the lip of the far side, and his motorcycle fishtailed violently one way, then the other—and it didn't stop. It was as if J.N. Roberts had been asked to describe a zigzag on the dry lake. The motorcycle continued to fishtail, and it was still going in a straight line at top speed, and I wondered why J.N. Roberts, the number one desert racer in the country, didn't seem to know what even *I* knew: he could stop the motorcycle from fishtailing if he just let off on the gas for half a second. And then it struck me: J.N. Roberts was number one because he would never let off on the gas for even half a second.

Next across came Rich Thorwaldson; his motorcycle dropped into the gully and came airborne out of the other side. He did just what I'd expected, and it was just as beautiful as I'd expected.

I was unimpressed. I wasn't even unimpressed. I was bored.

After fifteen or twenty expert racers came across the dry lake, I saw a hot-pink dot—Randy Milligan, an Invader! And after a few hundred more racers, before the gully became too much of a dust bowl, I saw another hot-pink dot—John McGowan and Kooky! I was amazed that as McGowan's motorcycle became airborne coming out, Kooky also became airborne for a moment: the tires of the motorcycle touched the lake bed just as Kooky's paws touched the carpeting gaffer's-taped to the gas tank.

Next came the novices, and it was uglier than I'd even hoped. One landed in the bottom and his motorcycle stopped solid, but the racer did not: he did an "endo"—flying end-over-end over the handlebars and landing on his ass in the sand. Another came by soon after and landed his motorcycle on top of the first one. Another racer sensed trouble ahead and laid his motorcycle down at high speed, then tumbled with it into the gully. After a few crashes, I began to lose interest, which was lucky since it had become too dusty to see anyway. I didn't wait around to try to see my brother come across the dry lake because I knew that even if I managed to see him in the dust and the wreckage, he'd just look like all these other poor suckers—the ones who weren't J.N. Roberts.

I rode back to the Invaders' camp, dropped off the binoculars, drank a cold soda, then practiced showing off by popping wheelies near the pits. But I couldn't stop thinking about J.N. Roberts, and how, by flying across a gully on a dry lake, he'd changed my life. His method of desert racing became my new philosophy. Because I understood, suddenly, that all of life's adversities could be overcome with one thing: velocity.

After my performance near the pits, I rode back to the Invaders' camp and waited for John to come in. I waited a long time. When I rode my Honda 55, I always wished

I had a faster motorcycle; now that I had a faster motor-cycle, I wished I had a faster brother.

When John did finally limp in on his jury-rigged Husqvarna 250, he was exhausted and bloodied—and elated. He took off his helmet and goggles, and his face, caked with dust, looked like a death mask. Tom Wise, one of the survivors of the superheated steam explosion at Edison's Mohave Generating Station, would describe the victims' faces the same way: "Their faces looked like death masks." But that day at the desert races, with fif-teen years of life ahead of him, my brother grinned as he cleaned the blood from his elbow and told me about the highlights of the race: the rocks, the dust, the racers everywhere, and the gully on the dry lake, where he'd crashed and got stuck.

"I finally had to hop off and *push* the bike out," he said, rightfully proud at finishing what was this sport's equivalent of the New York Marathon. All desert races were tough, but this one was especially so. Nearly half the field didn't even finish, and John had just beaten over a thousand racers. His finisher pin was already stuck to his dusty Invaders sweatshirt, displayed on his chest like one of the war medals he never got.

"But that gully was a killer," he said. "You couldn't even see as far as the *handlebars,* and it was hotter than *hell.*"

I smiled politely. Then I said, "Couldn't you have just gone *over* it?"

"Over . . . *what?*" he said.

"The gully," I said.

John nodded, obviously unhappy with his descrip-tion. He always took my questions seriously, even the dumb ones, and was endlessly patient with his answers. If I didn't understand something, he took it as a failing on his part. He broke off a stick from a nearby clump of sagebrush and began drawing a diagram in the sand.

"I know what it looks like," I said. "I saw it."

"Oh," he said, and stood, and waited.

"J.N. Roberts just flew *over* it—he didn't even let off on the gas."

John looked up, as if standing once again in the bottom of a dust-filled gully. "I guess it's possible," he said. "But by the time I got there, even if I did try to jump it, I couldn't see anything anyway."

"That's why you should go faster."

"What?"

"If you go faster, you won't be back in all the dust."

"If I go faster, I might crash."

"You crashed anyway," I said. "Why don't you just go faster?"

John tossed aside his stick. Then he shook his head and walked away from me. This would not be the last time he would walk away from me, nor the last time he would answer me with silence.

After he got out of the Marine Corps, John started working at our brother-in-law Ernie's bail bond office, just
across the street from the East L.A. sheriff station.

Between the bail bond office and the motorcycle
races, John evidently wasn't meeting too many eligible
women. So he said to his friends, "Don't you know any
women who are just normal? And nice?" I have no idea
what sort of relationships, good or bad, he'd already
gone through. John generally kept his romances well
away from his family, maybe because of what Joanne had
experienced because of Ernie. Our father was then
about midway through his decade of refusing to
acknowledge her, or Ernie's, existence.

John's friends said they knew just the woman, and
introduced him to Jeannie Eaton.

Jeannie wore cutoffs and tube tops, frosted lipstick
and loud sandals, and she had thickly mascara'd eye-
lashes. She had her own pool cue and, in the local bars,

knew how to use it. Jeannie exuded a kind of barroom cuteness, with an easy smile and an easier laugh. (My father, I found out much later, referred to Jeannie as "John's little tart," but he'd evidently learned to keep his opinions—his low ones anyway—to himself.) But what drew John to her, I suspect, is that she was in trouble: she'd been married to a bad man and now, thank god, was separated from him. She'd been staying with her sister, but even her sister was kicking her out. Jeannie didn't know *what* she was going to do.

John did. He paid for her divorce and told her to move in with him. I think John believed he was rescuing her, and that she was worth it. He told one of my sisters, "She's the only one in her family who hasn't joined the circus or been on welfare."

Still, John never really seemed happy in this scenario. He was often grim and morose when they'd come to my parents' house to visit, which was a weird contrast to Jeannie's easy laughter. But John had always been somewhat brooding, so he seemed mostly like himself, only a little more so.

Whatever action he'd missed in Vietnam, John's job made up for it.

The peak hours at a bail bond office are between midnight and six in the morning. But one quiet afternoon, while John was working alone, two men came into the office. One pulled out a gun and told John to hand over the money. John told him he didn't have any, that his boss had just come by and picked up all the cash. The gunman became frantic. He put the gun to John's temple and said, "Don't you understand, man, I'm gonna fucking kill you if you don't give me the money!" John maintained there wasn't any, and the gunman took John's wallet, his watch, and whatever else he had on him, then took John into a bathroom and handcuffed him to an exposed pipe.

After the gunman left, John hollered for help, but nobody heard him, so he picked up a metal trash basket and threw it through a high window. Somebody walking by heard the glass breaking, then heard John hollering and called the sheriff.

John was shaken after the holdup, but proud that he hadn't revealed to the gunman the thousands of dollars that were sitting in the safe. I'm not sure why he was so loyal to Ernie, except that it was simply John's nature to be loyal; in this way he was often hurt, and in this instance nearly killed.

Ernie was moving up in the world. He'd bought a liquor store in Montebello, and now John was needed there too. Ernie worked hard and did good business, some of it with the police officers he knew from his years as a bail bondsman. As a courtesy, Ernie would sell the cops a case of beer when they were still on duty, then leave it out back for them when he was closing so they could have a few beers at the end of their shifts. One night, while Ernie was ringing up their sale, the cops started teasing him about "his cutie over at the bank." Ernie began hissing at them, "Shhh! Shhh! That's my *brother-in-law* over there!" John, who was nearby stocking shelves, kept stocking.

Suddenly, John was really needed now at the bail bond office.

John had had some knowledge of all of this before—Ernie wasn't exactly subtle—but this was a different order of knowledge. That Ernie was screwing around was bad enough, but what made it worse was that he assumed John was a fool. He assumed Joanne was a fool as well. And in some ways he was right.

In high school, John had found himself in the sticky position of middleman—he couldn't stay friends with Richard Cannon and keep his other friends—and now he was in a much stickier position. Joanne had had two children by then: Michael, who was two, and Lisa, who wasn't yet one. If John told Joanne what he knew, it might mean the end of her marriage, her family, her happiness. If he didn't tell her, it might mean the end of her marriage, her family, her happiness.

So what John did was quit. Then he went to Joanne's house and told her what he'd long suspected and now knew for sure. He told her that Ernie was no good, and that she should leave him. (In his congenital bigotry, our father no doubt took some pleasure in this. He was raised about a dozen miles from the border, and in the days when he drove a truck and hauled hay, his skin was so dark that people often mistook him for a Mexican. But Ernie was a Mexican by blood and therefore no good.) Joanne said she couldn't leave Ernie; she had two little kids, and how would she take care of them? John told her that he'd take care of her and the kids—somehow. Just then, Ernie came home. He walked up to John and said, "Get out of my house, you fucking asshole." John looked at Joanne. I think he expected her to go with him, to leave right then, but she didn't. In an unfortunate choice of words, she told John, "Go, just go." Then she added, "It's okay." And John, freshly unemployed, probably feeling foolish, and certainly feeling humiliated, left.

That weekend, without telling anyone, John drove his girlfriend, Jeannie, to Las Vegas and got married.

I imagine he drove fast.

After John got married, we didn't go to the desert races very often. He got a new job delivering bottled water, and then, a few months later, moved up to Livermore, California, and got a job moving bombs at the naval shipyard in Oakland.

I got a job too, my first, at Lang's Dog Ranch, which was just up the road from my house. My chief responsibility was to handle everything that went into and came out of the dogs. But in addition to shoveling slop and picking up shit, I also got to wash and walk the dogs, and when the manager was out for the evening, I got to dog-sit in case of a fire or an emergency. This also allowed me to invite my buddies over to drink beer and smoke pot, which we did in stupefying quantities.

When John and Jeannie came down from Livermore, I regarded John as some sort of visiting incarnation of my father, which meant that I was cryptic and distracted and polite.

John and my father often worked out in the garage on one car or another, and Jeannie often helped in the kitchen, which my mother loved—not for the help but for the company. Jeannie would make her specialty, lemon pie from a mix, then add a few lemon seeds to make people think she'd baked it from scratch.

One day, she was making such a pie in front of Janice. My sister mentioned that she was looking for a new job, and Jeannie looked at her incredulously and said, "Why *work* when you can have a *man* take care of you?"

Midway through my alcoholic cruise through high school, I started training in Japanese karate, which I approached with the ferocity of my old hero J.N. Roberts. Suddenly I had something to be interested in, something to get better at, and I sailed through the ranks. My punches and kicks sounded like somebody snapping a gym towel. Soon I was teaching, competing in tournaments, and looking up to my new heroes, who could smash boards, bricks, bones.

When he came down to visit, I'd startle my brother with roundhouse kicks, which touched his ear softly as a kiss.

When I first got to Phoenix, the thought of food seemed a sickening reminder that my brother couldn't eat, couldn't move, and probably wouldn't even live. I got hungry anyway. I felt guilty for my hunger, guilty just for being alive, but I *was* alive, and to stay alive I had to eat.

The hospital cafeteria was downstairs, and for some reason, I usually got lost trying to find my way there or back. Sometimes I emerged from the hospital labyrinth only to find the cafeteria closed; it was open at fairly predictable hours, but I always managed to arrive a few minutes late. The burn unit did have a couple of vending machines, and I soon learned that the better machines, those with the freshest junk, were right next door, near the emergency room.

The ER was, by comparison with the burn unit, a lot more interesting, a lot less gloomy. Somebody was always wheeling in or limping out. There were lots of interesting wounds—arms bent at strange angles, tiny holes made by bullets, big slashes made by knives, colorful bruises and contusions—but all relatively cheerful stuff, being things that people could recover from.

Of course, lots of people probably died in the ER, yet death there—a swift death—seemed like a wild bit of good luck.

All of the patients in the ER, it seemed, had to wait, and what was further amazing was that every one of them watched TV. A disheveled businessman, a hard-worn young woman with a blackened eye, a tattooed gang member with a blood-soaked bandanna—they all stared up at one of the wall-mounted TVs, like faithful parishioners in the midst of a sermon.

Sometimes I sat with them, usually in the evening, when the news came on. Reports of the explosion at Southern California Edison's Mohave Generating Station—naturally big news in Arizona, California, and Nevada—were spreading nationwide. And for this, at least, I felt grateful.

The explosion was reported in the *Los Angeles Times* and the *New York Times*, and picked up by AP, UPI, and Reuters. The TV stations in Phoenix updated the conditions of the victims, and the networks were beginning to investigate how a disaster like this could have happened, and who was responsible. Those were questions we all wanted answered, and I knew that without the muscle of the press, they never would be.

I was watching the evening news in the ER one night, and the explosion at the Mohave Generating Station was in the list of teasers at the beginning of the national broadcast. *Good,* I thought. *I want the whole fucking world to know.*

Sitting next to me was a scraggly young man who looked to have been in a motorcycle accident. His face was scraped, one leg was twisted, and he stank of beer. "Hey, man," he said sadly.

"Hey," I said, then focused my gaze like a laser beam on the TV.

Halfway through the program, there was a special news bulletin: Iranian terrorists had hijacked a cruise ship called the *Achille Lauro,* and the early reports were that at least one passenger was dead.

The news anchor came back on to elaborate, and soon there was blurred footage and more information: the murdered passenger was a frail old man named Leon Klinghoffer, who'd been shot and then pushed overboard in his wheelchair.

That became, for the next few weeks, the *only* news story. One dead old man. In the explosion at Southern California Edison's Mohave Generating Station, sixteen people had been cooked alive; six finally died from thermal burns. The story was largely forgotten.

That evening in the ER, I sat stiffly through the broadcast. When it was over, I turned and looked at the young man next to me. He was, like everybody else, watching TV—not the news in particular, just whatever happened to be on. I looked at him, at all of them, and suddenly found no sympathy in my heart—not that there had been great reservoirs of it an hour before. I hated these slackers who inhabited the ER waiting room— feeling sorry for themselves and numbly watching TV. And I hated myself for doing exactly the same things.

I looked at this dipshit biker, and he looked back at me with his sad, pathetic eyes. I kept looking at him in a way that I'm sure was somewhat menacing, and he seemed to get a little worried. I didn't mind his discomfort. His scraped face would be bandaged, his broken bones set. He might suffer from recurring insurance problems, but his memories of this night would largely amount to a few scars, a limp, and a hangover. The son of a bitch would ride again. For some reason, though, he still seemed depressed, and I considered dragging his scraggly ass into the burn unit to help cheer him up.

My anger was becoming boundless. I hated my brother for not talking to me for five years, and I hated myself for going along with it. I hated him for dying. I hated my sisters for making a circus of his death. I hated the terrorists for hijacking that ship. I hated the media for dropping our story. And I even managed to hate Leon Klinghoffer for stealing the world's attention.

But in my heart I held a special hatred for Southern California Edison, and would have prayed that whoever was responsible for this disaster—this murder—would be consigned to the flames of hell except that those were surely cooler than the explosion of superheated steam at the Mohave Generating Station.

That anger has not abated.

After the news broadcast, I walked out of the ER, got in the rental car, and drove. I drove for a long time, my hands tight on the steering wheel. I shot ahead of any car that got too close, then turned abruptly onto streets with less traffic.

After a while I started getting hungry. The Mexican food in Phoenix is excellent, and I stopped for dinner at a seedy-looking place that reminded me of my favorite seedy-looking place in East L.A. I ordered the enchilada and chile relleno special—which seemed, from the age of the sign, to be a permanent special.

The man behind the counter said, "You want flour or corn tortillas with that?"

"What?" I said.

"Flour or corn," he said.

"Flour or corn," I repeated.

The man waited a moment, then said, "Mister, the tortillas, what do you want, flour or corn?"

"I want both," I said.

That evening, as we suited up to go into the burn unit, Al Laven told me, again, what a great guy my brother was. After training together, the two of them had even graduated on the same day. Et cetera.

Al was tying his surgeon's mask, which was bunched around his neck like a bandanna. "He'd come over for dinner at least once a week," he said, "and he really loved my kids. He was baby-sitting them just last week."

"Yes," I said. "I know." Then I said, "Did he ever say anything about me?"

Al stopped tying his mask and said, "Well, John said a lot of things."

At John's bedside, Al Laven spoke like the true friend he was. Neither shrill like Janice nor mindlessly optimistic like June, he remained just as steadfast in his belief that John was going to pull through.

John's chest rose and fell to the rhythm of the machine that pumped air into it. His swollen skin was red with splotches of yellow—places where it was turning septic fast and would have to be removed. More of his hair had been lopped off, to make the constant changing of tubes easier. On his forehead and neck, you could see bits of adhesive that the tape had left behind.

"You're gonna make it, buddy," Al told John.

It occurred to me that I'd never called my brother "buddy"—it was always something he'd called me. My brother had always been "John" or, when he was younger, "Johnny." I'd never called him "buddy" or "pal" or "bro." To call my brother anything but "John" would have been like calling my father "dude." It was just something I'd never thought to do, and just then, I wished I had. Because saying it before would have somehow given me permission to say it now—"Hey, buddy, I'm here with you"—but I didn't have that permission. I could only stand stiffly, speak stiffly, and watch somebody who did.

"You *gotta* make it, buddy," Al said, and smiled. "Who else am I gonna get to baby-sit?"

In the waiting room, I wondered just what my brother had said to Al Laven, and how much of it Al might tell me. Of course, that I had to ask somebody else about my brother's life—to ask somebody to tell me who my brother had become, and what he'd said, in particular, about me—was a stinging embarrassment.

What I wished to hear was obvious: "Yeah, John was sort of mad at you, but he always said he loved you."

Like many of my wishes in Phoenix, this one did not come true.

In some sense, I knew what the answers to my questions would be, but I asked anyway, hoping that I could at least steel myself in the midst of this tragedy; if my brother hated me so much, I could hate him back double, dismiss his suffering, even see it as something he deserved. I wished, very much, not to care.

This wish, too, did not come true.

"So," I said, "did John like it here?" Even though we were in Phoenix, "here" meant the desert, specifically the desert in Laughlin and Bullhead City, towns across from each other on the Colorado River; Laughlin is where John worked, and Bullhead City is where he wanted to live.

"Oh yeah, he loved it," Al said. "He'd already put a down payment on a lot in Bullhead City. He had the house all planned and everything. Right near my house. We'd get together and have dinner all the time. John wasn't into going out—bars, that sort of thing."

Al looked exhausted. Since the explosion, he'd become an emissary of goodwill for each of the burn victims—his friends, his coworkers—and had been driving back and forth among Phoenix, Laughlin, and Las Vegas, visiting burn units, visiting families, attending funerals.

"So, he lived in Bullhead City," I said, trying to construct my brother's life.

"Well, no, not yet," Al said. "He'd bought a trailer and lived in that out in Needles."

A trailer in Needles. Besides being a gas stop on Route 66, Needles, California, wasn't much more than a dismal speck of desert alongside the Colorado River. Living there would be bad enough, but living there in a trailer was worse. This fact didn't tell me anything about my brother—or if it did, it was nothing I wanted to know.

"You know," I said, "we hadn't talked for a long time."

Al shifted on the stiff couch.

"Five years," I said.

"Well," he said.

June was asleep on a nearby couch, her face dead white and deeply lined. Mom and Joanne and Janice had gone out for a while. It had gotten to a point where we all had to get out for a while.

"John was mad at everybody after his divorce," I said, and suddenly wished I hadn't. By saying this, it seemed, I was confirming everything my brother had probably told Al about me—that I wasn't a good brother, wasn't a good friend. "I tried to talk to him a lot of times," I blundered on, "but I don't even remember why he stopped talking to me." I could feel Al sizing me up, weighing the excuses of a lousy brother against the testimony of his best friend.

"Uh-huh," Al said.

We sat there and stared at June sleeping—her whole body clenched and twitching.

"I can't believe this is happening," I said. "It just isn't right."

"Yeah," Al said, "it never should have happened."

I wasn't sure just then whether Al meant the explosion or my falling-out with John.

"Hey," I said, and sat up. "Did John have a motorcycle?"

"A motorcycle?" Al said. "No, uh-uh."

"Oh," I said, and folded back in on myself.

When I was sixteen, I sold the Yamaha 125 that John had given me and bought a used Hodaka 100—a lightweight bike built for desert racing. The one I bought had already been raced a lot, and had been beat to shit, more or less. But I knew that a Hodaka was the right bike for me, the Yamaha being too heavy and not really a racing bike anyway. I needed a *racing* bike, even though we hadn't been to the desert races in months. And as it turned out, I'd never ride my Hodaka in the desert—in a race or otherwise.

Not long after I bought the Hodaka, June gave me her old car when she bought a new one. The car she gave me was a 1967 Ford Mustang—a gem except for its unfortunate color, a sort of metallic chartreuse with a matching alligator-patterned vinyl top. As soon as I could, I had it painted root-beer brown.

I also dismantled my Hodaka and painted the frame orange; a bright color, a fast color. The bike never even made it back together. I was too busy with my karate training to work on it, and didn't even know *how* to work on it. That was John and Dad's realm, not mine.

Once, when he'd driven down from Livermore for a visit, John saw the Hodaka in parts. He just shook his head and walked away.

He did the same a few months later. I'd sold the Mustang and bought a Sunbeam Tiger—a lightweight British sports car with a Ford V-8 engine. When it ran, the car could easily do 150 m.p.h. and burn rubber in all four gears. However, the Sunbeam seldom ran. It, like the Hodaka, was a piece of shit.

John looked the Sunbeam Tiger over.

"Want to drive it? It's pretty fast," I said, as if my brother needed a warning about fast cars.

John took the keys from me, and we went for a drive. He put the car through its paces—redlining the tach before shifting, attacking the turns, braking hard— which for me was a little frightening. I'd never ridden with John when he really pushed a car, especially *my* car, which had enough mechanical troubles just standing still. When John pulled up in front of the house, he made a point of parking on a clean patch of asphalt; he let the Sunbeam idle for a few minutes, then backed up. Even before I got out of the car, I could see the damning evidence on the asphalt—fresh oil spots—plain as chalk marks at a murder scene.

My next car, my next vehicle, was a used International Scout. I was opting for utility over speed, but my Scout provided neither. It looked like a four-wheel drive—it didn't occur to me that something so ugly wouldn't be a four-wheel drive—but it wasn't. It was noisy. It was slow. It handled like a banana boat. I once got it stuck on a steep driveway.

Then the engine block cracked. I didn't know how to fix it, and didn't even want to. I was done with high school by then, and I'd started working as a roadie for various rock bands, having started as a bodyguard. As a roadie, I drove a bobtail truck and set up the gear, and the first thing I'd do after renting a truck was unhook the governor, which regulated the speed. This allowed me to haul ass from one gig to the next, even though the trucks sometimes suffered. Once, while driving through Arizona, I literally blew the side out of an engine. No matter—the rental company had a new truck for me in a few hours. I prided myself on being a mover, not a fixer.

I wasn't in Los Angeles very often, and when I was, I usually had a rental car. We were—my road buddies and I—hard on rental cars, but I pushed my abuses to a point that, I think, appalled even them. Oh, I went through the usual bumper-car routines with them, but I would also throw an automatic transmission into park while driving on the freeway (the transmission makes a sound like a stick dragged across a picket fence), and I had perfected a maneuver called a Power Reverse: while driving forward, I would let off on the gas for a moment, then throw the automatic transmission into reverse, and the tires would spin and smoke as the car slowed. A Power Reverse is best achieved at speeds under thirty miles an hour, and I speak from experience. I once dropped a transmission in a Ford station wagon while performing a Power Reverse.

The International Scout sat broken on my parents' driveway while I was on the road, until the day John and my father decided to fix it. They took the engine apart, and John did what he could to rebuild the block, but there wasn't much to work with. They got it running, though, my arthritic father and my overworked brother, and I came home that day and found them putting my latest mistake back together, fixing it, while I sat there helpless on my fancy Halliburton luggage and watched.

. . .

Every day, John's condition steadily worsened. The Death Summary reads, "His hospital course was one of a progressively downhill course."

I was still haunted by what John had said when I first got to Phoenix, or what he'd tried to say—whatever it was, I didn't understand. *I want you know* . . . know what? Know what I really think of you? *I want you both* . . . to get out? And it was becoming clear that those words would probably be his last, and whatever their meaning, I'd missed it.

John was on dialysis because his kidneys couldn't handle the massive infection from the burns, but even this wasn't working. The doctors, to their credit, always had another procedure, another drug, another way to try and save the human machine—my brother's life—while I stood by numbly and watched.

When John and Jeannie finally moved back to Southern California, John bought a half interest in an engine-rebuilding shop in El Monte. They lived out in Yucaipa, about an hour's drive outside Los Angeles. Neither place, from my perspective, had much to recommend it. El Monte was an industrial suburb of Los Angeles, and Yucaipa was an agricultural suburb of nowhere.

I was living in Santa Barbara for a while, and then in Laguna Beach—both tony beach towns—and soon I would be living in a big glitzy house in the Hollywood Hills.

One day, when I'd just flown into town from a tour, I drove out to my brother's shop and said hello, and glanced around his shop, then drove off in my new convertible, my shiny Halliburton briefcase on the seat beside me.

My brother was probably proud to show me around, but as I walked through his shop, what impressed me most was my ability to weave through it without brushing against anything and getting grease on my designer jeans. In my brother's world, people bought new engines. In my world, people bought new cars.

Before leaving, I picked up one of my brother's business cards from the front desk and noticed that his name read JOHN DOLEN. When I pointed out the misspelling, my brother nodded and let out a little snort, and told me his business partner had ordered the cards. Clearly, John was pissed off about the mistake, but I was amazed that he'd let it stand. I dealt with dozens of people every day—promoters, hotel managers, union bosses—and didn't hesitate to jump in the face of anybody who fucked up.

I knew my brother had been having some troubles with Jeannie—they were separated—and I stared at his business card and told him he should drive down and visit me in Laguna Beach, get some sun, hang out, but what I was thinking was, *Pathetic.*

One of the truck drivers from the tour I'd just been on had given me a sheet of acid—twenty or thirty tabs of tiny eyes printed on an index-card-sized piece of paper. He'd warned me about the acid, which I'd never taken before—not that it might be too strong, but too weak. "You might need to take a few," he'd said.

So I took a few hits that night. All of my road buddies happened to be out of town, so I was lonely and feeling sorry for myself. My brother had left a message for me, but I didn't think he'd cheer me up, and thought he could only make it worse; he'd been miserable about

Jeannie. I didn't feel the acid that night, and finally fell into an uneasy sleep. I woke up very early and figured, what the hell, I might as well see what acid's really like, and took a few more hits.

I went out to breakfast at the Bakery. This was Flag Day, 1979. Nixon was out of office but still living down in San Clemente, and I read something about him in the *Los Angeles Times* and started laughing loudly. Very loudly. I took a few more hits—half the sheet, in fact. I figured everybody was laughing along with me about Nixon. Then, as soon as the camera shop across the street opened for business, I reeled over and bought one of the first automatic-everything cameras; you could be on acid and take photographs with this thing—and I have two rolls to prove it.

My logic for the day was to make the police so paranoid they'd leave me alone. This seemed to work. The first shots on the roll are of the woman who was selling me the camera, and then a snapshot of a meter maid. Then there's a photograph of my side-view mirror (I was driving), in which a police cruiser is framed. There's a photograph of a police officer directing traffic, and a blurred picture of lizards in a pet shop, and one of beautiful twin girls, looking stunned at the acid-crazed man who insisted on taking their picture.

Sometime after the pet shop and the tourist girls, the world began to swirl and melt. Somehow, I drove home and managed to open the door before puking and falling down face-first into the mess.

I lay there for hours, comatose and yet *aware* that I was comatose. I figured I was going to die, and even thought, *Oh shit, I'm going to die here like this in a pool of puke.* I couldn't move my head; I was paralyzed and drug-numb, but my heart was beating fast as a jackrabbit's.

I fell asleep, and when I woke up I still couldn't move, and I thought, well, this is it, and then realized I couldn't move not because I was paralyzed but because the puke around my head had dried. My head was stuck to the carpet.

I pulled free with a kind of *thwuck* and went into the bathroom and cleaned up. I walked around the house for a while. I checked my phone messages. My brother had called again—evidently he'd driven down to Laguna, just as he'd said he would, but I didn't seem to be around. Then I remembered the camera! There were two exposures left, so I took a picture of myself in the bathroom mirror—my head is, appropriately enough, a flash of light—and then I drove to the tiny photo developing booth down in South Laguna. I placed the camera on top of my car for the last picture, set the timer. That picture shows a very tired young man standing in front of a very beautiful Pacific Ocean at sunset.

John did drive down to Laguna again—and this time I made a point of being ready. I'd told each of my road buddies, who were over for a barbecue, that my older brother was coming and to try to act normal, don't do any drugs in his presence, preferably don't do any drugs anyway, and don't even smoke any pot. ¸

It was more like I was preparing for my grandmother's visit.

I said hello to John and looked around to see who I might introduce him to. I thought my brother might have something in common with one of my road buddies, Woody, who'd also been in the Marine Corps.

Woody was a large black man and a legendary roadie. He used to get drunk after gigs and, for fun, pick me up over his head and run across the empty stage.

Woody was also a great driver—and this, I figured, would cinch things with John. Woody had been stationed in El Toro, California, where his commanders had evidently noticed his driving skills, and he was put on call to drive President Nixon whenever he was down in San Clemente. He'd driven Nixon a few times in the course of things—not very often. It was a job that allowed him a great deal of time to goof off. One night, Woody got The Call. Unfortunately, he'd dropped acid a few hours earlier. He went anyway, and drove flawlessly—Nixon in the back, a pistol strapped to the inside of the driver's door, Woody at the wheel on acid.

Actually, Woody told me he drove Nixon on acid *twice*.

I looked around the room and saw all of my road buddies—all people who smoked pot and snorted cocaine and drank anything and everything and then chased pussy and traveled on. They were all, in other words, like me.

I steered John away from Woody and introduced my brother to a good-looking woman, then nervously wandered off. The next time I saw her, she was out on the porch smoking a joint. I rushed over and said, "Uh, my brother's here."

"Yeah, I met him a little while ago," she said. "We talked for a long time. He's a cool guy."

I thought she was joking. "Would you mind putting out the joint?" I said.

Each time my brother started talking to somebody new, I'd hurry over and try to make sure the conversation didn't veer into the wrong topic. Drugs, sex, rock 'n' roll—I didn't think my brother would approve.

I wanted to present a neat little normal life to my brother. I wanted him to come down and have a pleasant visit, see that I was normal, that my friends were normal—look at how normal we all are!—then leave and get back to his normal life. I wanted to present him with a postcard of my life, something glossy and pretty that he could take home with him.

I probably thought of him more as a father than as a brother, but through my caricature of sonlike respect, I treated him as less than a brother, and certainly as less than a friend.

After they separated, John spoke bitterly of Jeannie and her deceptions, sometimes talking to one of our sisters halfway through the night while he vented his rage. Which made it all the more difficult for him when he and Jeannie got back together. When I saw the two of them, it was hard not to see in her friendly smile the leer of the demon he'd described. No matter—it didn't last long.

After the divorce, John moved back into our parents' house, which he left each day to go to work at his engine-rebuilding shop, and which he came home to each day after work, whereupon he'd lie on his bed and smoke Marlboros, drink diet Pepsis, and watch TV. This lasted two years, during which John's cynicism and anger flourished. He stopped talking to me. He stopped talking to Joanne. If he spoke to anyone, it was himself, and he spoke only of anger.

He seemed consumed by it—and six years later, as I stood beside his hospital bed in the Maricopa County Medical Center, as I looked at his burn-swollen skin, I was struck by the notion that John's body had merely taken longer to catch up with the white-hot anger in his heart.

The doctors had had John on dialysis for a week but his kidneys were still failing, as were his lungs, which were burned badly and now had pneumonitis. The doctors explained to us the gravity of the situation—the man was dying—but June heard only that his kidneys were failing, and offered one of her own.

The doctors shook their heads; such a transplant wouldn't even be remotely possible with someone in his condition. Then they went on with the list of procedures they'd follow next, knowing full well that it would be a useless, valiant effort, but also knowing that my sisters would accept nothing less.

In the waiting room, I couldn't stop thinking about June offering one of her kidneys; it was like offering a drowning man Kleenex, and it angered me that she'd do something to prolong his suffering, and that she'd risk her own life while doing it. Our mother might lose two children instead of one. It also angered me that I hadn't offered a kidney, and that I wasn't sure, even if John were in otherwise good health, that I would have.

June was not, of course, trying to prolong his suffering—she wanted to save his life—but this is the way I saw it: John was dying, and no medicine, no kidney, no goodwill, and no prayer would bring him back. He was on his way, and I wanted to speed him on his journey. I was also terrified by the thought of my brother alive: burned in places to the bone, deeply scarred, crippled, and forever angry at me, if not for my failures before the explosion, then for my failures after—his anger pumping through a kidney I hadn't even thought to offer.

Four or five days before he died, it became clear that John was going to, but because of my sisters' steadfast belief otherwise, the doctors told us only what procedures they were taking to save his life and, if those failed, the procedures they'd take next. They didn't mention the gross mutilation that prolonging his life required—and how could they have? Which of my sisters would have listened?

Because the doctors were working on John more often, we didn't have as many opportunities to visit. That's what we still called it, "a visit," though all I did was stand beside his bed and watch the machines regulate and monitor his life, and all my sisters did was talk as if nothing had happened that couldn't somehow unhappen.

I shuffled out of John's room (shuffled because of the paper slippers that covered my shoes). My sisters were still inside, and Janice's voice filled the burn unit. It embarrassed me, her voice—even with our brother dying. I lingered near the nurses' station and waited until all of my sisters had left. As they were walking out, I heard Janice say, "I think he's looking better."

Before taking off my paper gown and cap and slippers, I stopped by Dr. Stein's office, letting my surgeon's mask hang from my neck like a pro. Another doctor was in the office with him.

Dr. Stein's office was small, windowless, and uncluttered, the office of a man who rarely had time to sit in it.

"I wanted to ask you about my brother's condition."

"Fine," he said. "Do you mind if Dr. McGeever is here, or would you rather talk to me in private?"

"No, he's fine," I said. I did want to talk to Dr. Stein in private, and by private I meant without my family.

I took a deep breath and said, "Look, he's going to die, right?"

I noticed on Dr. Stein's desk a box of doughnuts, brightly glazed and sprinkled, and two Styrofoam containers with lids. For some reason, I found this fascinating—here, men who save lives, eating crap.

Dr. Stein didn't hesitate. "Yes," he said.

Dr. McGeever explained what they'd lately tried, and the unsuccessful results.

I said, "So there's not any hope of a miracle?"

"No," Dr. Stein said.

I heard what Dr. Stein had said, but I needed more to go on in order to make this clear to my sisters. I said, "So it's not a question of 'if' but 'when'?"

"That's right," he said.

I knew John was dying, but the absolute certainty of it stalled me; to some extent, I still wanted to believe Janice and June's cheers, their dreams of speedy recovery.

"Is this the right time to talk about taking him off of life support?" I said.

"Yes," Dr. Stein said.

"Then, can we take him off life support?" I said.

"No," Dr. Stein said. "Legally, we can't do that. We can stop any *further* procedures, but we can't take him off of anything we've already started."

I was sick and exhilarated. "Then can we stop any further procedures?"

"Yes," he said. "All you have to do is get your family to agree to it."

I looked at Dr. Stein and laughed. "Is *that* all?" I said. The thought of my family agreeing on *anything* was ridiculous, but the thought of them agreeing on *this* was stupefying.

"We can talk to them, if you'd like."

"You can try," I said. "I mean, there's no hope, right?"

"Not really," he said.

"He *is* going to die," I said.

Dr. Stein and Dr. McGeever looked at me. I looked at the doughnuts.

"We'll talk to them," Dr. Stein said.

"If all we're doing now is prolonging his suffering . . ." I said.

"We'll talk to them," Dr. McGeever said.

"Instead of his life."

The doctors nodded.

I got up, lifted my paper sleeve, and wiped my face. I thanked them, and just as I was about out the door I stopped and said, "Has anybody told him?"

"Told who?" Dr. Stein said.

"Told John," I said.

"What?" Dr. Stein said.

"Has anybody told him that he's going to die?"

Dr. Stein looked at Dr. McGeever. Then he looked at me. "No," he said.

"Shouldn't he know what's happening to him?" I said. "Do you think somebody should tell him he's going to die?"

Dr. Stein got up, put his hand on my shoulder, and said, "I think somebody should tell him."

Al Laven was back in the waiting room, and he'd brought with him a bunch of John's coworkers, mostly men and a few women, who had driven down from Laughlin or Bullhead City. They came to offer support for John and our family, but they also came to see for themselves what had happened; after all, this could have been any one of them. They also seemed to come out of a purely human curiosity about death, to see what death was, and they spoke as if John was already dead.

I was sober and purposeful as I walked back into the waiting room. I wasn't interested just then in meeting John's coworkers; I didn't have the energy to go through my muted grief with them, and didn't want to hear theirs. But they needed to talk about the explosion, to try to make sense of it themselves, just as Al Laven had when we got here, and just as I am doing now.

Each of them had to tell us what a great guy John was, and though I know they were sincere and meant this in the kindest way possible, for us it was just another painful reminder of what we were losing with his death.

I talked to one man who told me how bad the explosion had been, how the reheat pipe had been blown backward from the blast, how it had blown down the wall to the lunchroom and what damage it had done inside. He'd worked with John, and it was clear from the way he was talking that he could just as easily have been in that bed in this burn unit, and that in coming here to face John's death, he was also facing his own.

"We need to talk to the doctors," I said to Joanne, and she nodded, as if she'd been expecting this. I told June and my mom, and they nodded wearily, as if this was just another nameless stage of a nightmare they could not wake from.

"We need to talk to the doctors," I said to Janice. She had her knees tucked under her and was turned toward one of John's coworkers, a man who was telling her about the specifics of the blast.

"I was on the crew that went in there after it happened," the man said, "and it was unbelievable. Everything was melted—you could see the marks on the side of the horseshoe where they tried to get away. The marks were from their skin."

We were all listening to him, and my mother let out a deep sigh and stood up; she couldn't listen to any more.

"Janice," I said, "we need to talk to the doctors. We need to have a family meeting."

Janice was looking at the man and twirling a lock of her hair. She looked at me as if I'd just interrupted an intimate moment. "Jay," she said, "I'm *visiting*." To some extent, it seemed that Janice, too, had been expecting this meeting, but she still wanted to avoid it.

"It's important," I said.

Janice stood and apologized in a tone suggesting that once she had tended to the goofy whims of her little brother, they could resume the serious matter of their conversation.

I sensed lines were already being drawn. If I was going to have to negotiate my brother's death, I was on the side of betrayal and godlessness (because I did not hold to an obstinate belief in a miracle), and my sister Janice would represent loyalty and hope.

"They need to talk to us," I said to my mother, and she pulled her sweater up over her shoulders and nodded gravely. My mother had no illusions about what this meeting might be about.

"What?" June said. "What?" Her face was pale and puffy. She'd also been talking to one of the men from the Mohave plant, but she seemed barely able to concentrate. "I wish people would tell me what's going on," she said.

"The doctors need to talk to us," I said. "We need to talk to them."

I thought Joanne would be my best hope in recruiting an ally. As we walked toward the burn unit, I held one of Mom's arms and Joanne held the other; I talked to her over my mother's fine white hair. "He's just suffering, Jo," I said. "There's nothing they can do for him. I asked the doctors, and they told me. What kind of life could he have anyway? We can't just let him keep suffering, we've got to do something."

"Has his condition changed?" Janice said. Her voice was accusatory and sharp. This was her normal voice.

"His condition changed?" June said.

"No," I said, "his condition hasn't changed."

"Then what's the *problem*?" Janice said.

"I wish somebody would tell me when there's a problem," June said.

I started to answer but my voice—my whole body—was weighted with dread.

Joanne held Mom's arm a little tighter as we neared Dr. Stein's office, and I did the same.

We sat in Dr. Stein's office, and I thought of the time ten months earlier when we'd sat in the mortician's office at Rose Hills and attended to the business of my father's burial.

About five years earlier, my father had gone into the hospital for some minor surgery on his arthritic hands, and then he suffered a heart attack, then another, and then was taken into surgery for abdominal pains. I was there for that one; it got worse day by day, and I sat in the waiting room and waited for him to die. I was there with my mother when the doctor came out of surgery and gave us the news that my father had made it but the prognosis was grim. The doctor told us he'd had to remove 90 percent of my father's large intestine. The doctor's first language was not English, and when he had trouble explaining to my horrified mother what had happened, he said "Wait" and went back into the surgery room. He came back out with a big stainless steel bowl, and in it was something large and dark and coiled—not unlike the big rattlesnakes my father used to kill in the San Diego Mountains. The doctor said,

"The blood clot . . ." and my mother said, "Oh no," and turned away.

The Styrofoam cups, half empty now, were still on Dr. Stein's desk, but the empty doughnut box and waxed paper were sticking out of the wastebasket. Dr. Stein wiped something from his lips, then sat on the edge of his desk. "This is Dr. McGeever," he said.

I'd hoped that Dr. Stein would simply lay out the facts—professionally, dispassionately—and that my family would then see clearly what needed to be done. From the start, I'd questioned the viability of John's life, and what kind of life he might live, and whether or not he'd want to live it. There were times during the last two weeks that I'd wished him dead—an impulse that started with love, looped around to anger, and ended up back at love again. To desire his death seemed humane, because what we were extending now was not his life but suffering, both his and our own.

Dr. Stein began to tell my family exactly what he'd told me: that John was in all likelihood not going to make it, that the burns to his skin were bad enough on their own, but his lungs were also burned, his kidneys had shut down . . .

As Dr. Stein was talking, I realized that the same things he'd just said to me sounded different now, because the audience was different. My mother and Joanne seemed to hear what I'd heard, but I could sense June's absolute bafflement. She was in no way prepared for a discussion about John's death, and certainly not for one about hastening it. I didn't understand how June could have failed to see in his tortured body what was obvious to me, although the obvious, I was beginning to realize, was relative; we each saw and heard what we wanted, or what we were able to want.

"What are you going to do next?" Janice said, more of a challenge than a question.

"Well," Dr. Stein said, "that's what we need to discuss."

I could see just where this conversation was heading.

"As I told J.D., we can't take him off of life support, but we can stop any further procedures, if that's what you want."

Janice rose like a prize rooster and said, "All I've got to say is I want you to do everything you can to save *my* brother's life!" Her voice was breaking, and she turned and walked out of the office.

June said, "Is there *any* hope that he could live?"

Dr. Stein said, "Well, there's always a possibility . . ."

"There could be a miracle?" June said, as if granting her permission to arrange one.

"Well, it would take a miracle."

"We're just making him suffer longer," I said, although I knew that with Janice's theatrical exit, there was no way now to talk about what was best for John.

"If there's a chance for a miracle," June said, "then I think we've got to keep trying. I just can't agree to end his life if there's any hope. There could be a miracle; I know there could be a miracle."

Dr. Stein nodded, not in agreement, exactly, but in recognition of having gone through this before.

My mother said, "I know there's no hope, but I can't take any fighting. I just can't. I guess keep trying for now."

Joanne nodded and said, "For now."

I was the last of my family to walk out of the office, and I thanked Dr. Stein for trying.

"I'm sorry," he said, "but unless everybody agrees."

"Yeah, I understand," I said.

"We'll keep his medications up," he said. "And don't worry. It won't be long."

I walked out of the office and down the corridor toward the waiting room. My mother and sisters were sitting with John's coworkers again, and I didn't even glance in their direction as I walked past. I didn't want to talk to them, any of them. I heard someone—Al Laven, I think—start to say my name and stop before he got to the D. I didn't care if I looked like the kind of shitty, self-centered brother that John had probably portrayed. Because, just then, that whole group of exhausted, teary-eyed people—my mother, my sisters, his friends—were either part of the sinister forces who had killed my brother or part of the sinister forces who were keeping him alive.

I put on my Vuarnet sunglasses, the automatic doors slid open, and I stepped out into the burning world.

I drove. I don't remember in which direction, or how long, only that every once in a while the Maricopa County Medical Center would suddenly be looming in my windshield again, reminding me that I had gone, and was going, nowhere.

My sisters, I knew, were not on some evil mission to lengthen John's suffering. They loved their big brother and they wanted him to live, period. They would concern themselves later with the quality of that life. Right now, they wanted him to stage a miracle, shake it off, wake up grinning. They wanted him to win.

Still, the man was dying. His kidneys were shutting down, his lungs, his heart. Nobody had told him this, and it's unlikely he could have heard much anyway; in addition to his body shutting down, his veins were—thank god—coursing with morphine. If he'd heard anything, it was probably his sisters' shrill and best-intentioned chorus: YOU'RE LOOKING BETTER, JOHN! YOU'RE GONNA MAKE IT!

He was not looking better. He was not going to make it.

I thought about the first time I'd had to deal with death, and how John was there to ease me through it. I'd had a dog, a terrier mix named Ferndock (Glen Burbank, Joanne's boyfriend and John's DeMolay friend, suggested that as a joke, but I loved the name so much that, against my parents' wishes, it stuck). Ferndock was not a smart dog. He chewed on the lawn furniture, barked a lot, and, whenever he had the chance, would run out into the street. Once he ran out and got hit by a car. He came limping back to the house, badly hurt. His body looked bent. Blood dribbled from his mouth. John wrapped Ferndock in a packing blanket and took him to the vet. When John came back, alone, a few hours later, I asked him if Ferndock was going to be all right, and he said no, the vet had to put him to sleep. I figured this meant a nap, and asked him when Ferndock would wake up. John had me sit on the porch, and then he sat down beside me. He told me that Ferndock had died because he was hurt too badly. I asked why the vet didn't do an operation, do something to save him, and John told me, again, that the dog was hurt very badly, and that even if he lived he'd always be in a lot of pain, and he asked me if I wanted Ferndock to be in a lot of pain. I wept and said no, but there must have been *something* the vet could've done, and John said the vet *did* do something, he made it so Ferndock wouldn't hurt anymore.

John could have told me anything, but he'd told me the hard truth, so I came to understand truth as generous and kind as well as very often painful in the telling and the hearing. I also came to understand that my brother would never lie to me.

For me to tell John that he was going to die—although I had no idea what he'd do with the information—now seemed essential. I also had no idea how to tell him, or *what* to tell him.

We'd never been a religious family. My mother had taken me to church now and then, since our next-door neighbor was a tyrannical Baptist preacher who occasionally had loud battles with his kind wife, Pearl. I remembered exactly nothing from my church experiences, except that in Sunday school I'd won a contest for reciting the names of the books of the New Testament (*Matthew, Mark, Luke, John, Acts, Romans, Apostles . . .*) and that the prize was a model car my brother helped me build.

As I drove, I started composing what I might say to John. I was, after all, a writer now—or I would be as soon as the *Mississippi Review* came out—and whatever I said, it seemed important to say it right.

Nothing sounded right.

To invoke God and heaven seemed wrong—a quieter and more reverent version of my sisters' cheerleading. I might believe in a spirit or gods or even *a* god, but not in the form of the plastic Jesuses poised on half the heat-scorched dashboards in Phoenix. And neither heaven nor hell was waiting after death, but a way of thinking during life.

As to God, I couldn't imagine any omnipotent being delivering this kind of agony upon anyone so innocent—and if there was such an omnipotent, then God and Job and Job's Daughters be damned.

I had to tell him he was going to die, and a few other things along with it, because it occurred to me that just hearing that he was going to die—the final realization—might kill him.

Janice and June came back to the waiting room from the burn unit; Joanne and I could go in now. We took turns, usually in this pairing. It was an awful burden, just going in there, but it seemed like we had to do it.

I still didn't know how I was going to tell John, and there wasn't much of him left to tell, and there wouldn't be long to tell it. Joanne and I just stood by his bed and gripped the rails and stared.

She said, "Hello, John."

I said, "Hi, John."

We stood there for a long time.

"See you in a while, John," Joanne said.

"See you . . ." I said, and choked on the words I couldn't get out.

We stood near the entrance, taking off our protective clothing—our baby blue paper smocks, our paper caps, our surgeon's masks now routinely kept around our necks. We were shedding this stuff, throwing it away.

I said, "I just wish I knew what he'd said when we got here." I waited for a moment, hoping Joanne would offer a guess, but she didn't. "I mean, I don't think he's going to say anything else. It was something like, 'I want you know . . .' or 'I want you both . . .' Maybe he wanted me to know he was still pissed off at me. Jesus, maybe he wanted *both* of us to get out."

Joanne pulled off her surgeon's mask and just stared at me.

"He was trying to say *something*," I said.

"He wasn't *trying* to say something. He said it."

"Maybe it was, 'I want you . . . know . . .' Know what?"

Joanne put her hand on my shoulder, and spoke softly, so I might better read her lips: "What he said was, *I love you both.*"

I sat in the hotel bar that night, slugging down single-malt scotch and writing lines in my notebook and then crossing them out.

I know you've been mad at me for a long time, and I'm sorry.

Sorry? Sorry for what? For being young and stupid? I was sorry for acting badly, but I was sorrier that he'd judged me so harshly, the son of a bitch, sorry that he lived so many years in bitterness and anger and distrust.

John, I want you to know I forgive you.

I imagined my brother rising from the bed like a monster from a horror film. Forgive him? I couldn't imagine that John would want my forgiveness.

You have to prepare yourself, John, you're not going to make it.

I had no clue how one might prepare for this—and then wondered if the very notion of telling him was more for my benefit than for his. He might be drugged enough to slip quietly away, and my testimony might only cause spasms of fear and panic.

I knew he deserved to know the truth, and that I had to tell him—mainly because nobody else was about to.

John, you're going on a journey . . .

John, I know I've done a lot of things wrong . . .

John, I know you've done a lot of things wrong . . .

John, I'm sorry we've grown apart, but . . .

John, I want you to know what's happening, I know you'd tell me the truth, and I want to tell you the truth . . .

John, it's Jay. I've got to tell you something . . .

I was getting nowhere. To give him an accurate clinical description of what was happening seemed important, since the doctors hadn't told him anything and all he'd heard from my sisters was their wishes, which had little to do with his truth. But it was painful to speak in clinical terms about what was rapidly becoming a spiritual event. John was at the threshold of life's greatest mystery, and outside of my ability to recite *Matthew, Mark, Luke* . . . I had no language with which to talk to my brother about what might come next—and between us, I realized, this was nothing new.

John, I'm sorry, I'm so sorry . . .

He was dying. He needed to know that. He needed to know what had happened, and what was happening, and what was going to happen. I could do that. I would just have to talk to him man to man. But how would I talk to him like a man when all I'd ever been was his little brother? I hadn't known my brother for years, nor had he known me. I still thought of John in his red Corvette; I thought of him in pegged slacks and alpaca sweaters, his hair slicked back with Vitalis. I didn't know who my brother was anymore—didn't even know what kind of car he drove.

The cocktail waitress came over and set down another glass of scotch. "This one's on me," she said. I raised my head, probably for the first time in about an hour, and looked at her. She had short brown hair and light green or light blue eyes, and she was smiling.

"Thanks," I said.

"You look busy," she said.

"Oh, this?" I said, closing the notebook. "What's your name?"

She told me, then said, "So what do you do?"

"Me?" I said, and suddenly got this heady feeling that wasn't just from the scotch. "I'm a writer."

The next morning, I woke up with a hangover. In my shirt pocket, there was a matchbook with a woman's name and a phone number. Whatever notes I'd written had been torn from the notebook and, apparently, thrown away.

The waiting room was becoming claustrophobic. We'd been there nearly two weeks, probably more time than we'd spent together in the last two years.

My brother was dying. My sisters' brother, my mother's son. We sat staring deep into ourselves, trying to grasp that this was really happening. We didn't even try to conceal our stunned and widening grief. And yet, at the same time, we were tired of grief itself; it covered us like a blanket that we sometimes had to shrug off, laughing at the slightest opportunity, whether or not anything was funny. "Oh, I *thought* that coffee tasted a little strange," my mother said after sipping a cup of Coke, and we all laughed for a moment and stretched our muscles before the grief settled back onto us, darkening our eyes and pressing our shoulders into a hunch.

My mother didn't go into the burn unit very often now. Even Joanne was showing the strain. Al Laven, though, was a man transformed by this experience, positively: he'd driven back and forth from Laughlin, from Las Vegas, and spent time with a lot of the families of the blast victims. In the aftermath of the blast, he'd done everything he could to help everybody he could. His friendship and faith were unshakable.

I found it a bit much.

At first, Al had been as angry as any of us about the blast. He'd drawn diagrams for me, detailed the shoddy conditions of the plant and Southern California Edison's criminal disregard for its workers. But now he was suddenly circumspect. Edison was keeping him on full salary as he made his goodwill missions; back home he was part of the team that was cleaning up the aftermath, and would be part of the team that would rebuild the Mohave Generating Station. He was no less damning of what had happened, but the "they" who had caused the catastrophe were now a "we" who would never let such a thing happen ever again. He spoke with bitterness and conviction. He offered to lead us in prayer again. He was getting paid for it.

I decided to go for a drive.

．　．　．

I thought about Al Laven and how John's death was becoming a defining moment in his life, and how it was also becoming a defining moment in mine. I wondered if I should've had more faith—blind, stupid, or otherwise—like Janice and June. I wondered if my faith would've made a difference.

In some ways, I was glad that his death would hide the rift between us. With John dead, I thought, I wouldn't have to go through the sticky reality of talking through it with him, wouldn't have to admit my bad behavior or his, wouldn't have to struggle to be friends again. I was wrong about his death hiding the rift between us, of course, and everything else.

I stopped for lunch at the same little Mexican restaurant I'd been to before and ordered the special, with corn tortillas, then sat down to write the end of my brother's life.

John, you need to know this . . .

The booth I was sitting in was covered with vinyl; it was cool and, in places, sticky. I drank bad iced water from a big plastic glass. I could hear a cook in the kitchen working a knife against a cutting board. All this—sticky vinyl and bad water and the sounds of somebody cooking—reminded me that I was alive, and that life seemed very precious. I drank the bad water like fine wine, and when the waitress brought my food out and said, "Watch the plate, it's hot," I think she thought I was hitting on her.

A TV was mounted on the wall, and though it must have been on since I walked in, I only just then noticed it. At the end of a Spanish-language program, the news was such that language was irrelevant; the newscaster was doing the weather—the high, the low, the sunrise, the sunset—and I realized that today was the summer solstice, the longest day of the year. Except what I thought about was how every day would now be getting shorter.

John had had a seizure just the day before. He didn't have much time left, and I didn't have much time left to tell him. I left some money on the table, on top of the grease-stained check, took a last long drink of bad water, then ran out to my rental car expecting that it might already have happened, that I'd failed my brother first in life and now in death.

In the waiting room, nothing had changed. Al Laven sat there with my mother and my sisters. I sat beside them, and set to work once again on the text that might tell me how to tell my brother he was going to die.

"Are you going back to New York soon?" my mother said.

"After the funeral," I said, and immediately felt bad for saying it. I wasn't worried about my mother—she just nodded sadly—but about Janice and June, who both seemed to think that John's imminent death was a matter of opinion.

"Well, I still think ol' John could pull through," Al said. "When I was in there earlier this morning, I think he could hear me." This wasn't a flat-out contradiction of the obvious—just a bit of hopeful bait for my sisters.

I also took the bait. "You *think* he heard you?" I was still tired from my hangover, nearly ready for some contorted sleep on the stiff couch, but suddenly I felt alert and actually interested in what he had to say. I knew the basis of his statement was probably untrue, but some inadvertent truth might have slipped in. When I first came to Phoenix, I wondered if my brother could speak, and now I wondered if he could hear; everything in me was speeding up. I leaned forward intently, and listened.

"Well," Al said, "it's hard to tell. But I was talking to him, telling him he was going to make it, and I said, 'I know you're gonna make it, buddy,' and John seemed like he tried to move his hand."

"Tried to," I said.

"Well, moved it," he said. "A little."

Janice and June took this as a certified miracle. "I knew it!" Janice said. "See?" June said to me, and her smile revealed the teary puffiness around her eyes. Joanne smiled grimly. My mother smiled too, though so briefly that it could easily have been missed.

The "buddy" issue still pained me, but I really wanted to believe that John could hear something, anything, or that, perhaps, he could still hear me. I didn't believe my words might make him well, only that, if I could find the right words, he might die without hating me. Or himself.

"Are you going to use the car for a while?" Janice said. She seemed buoyed by Al's positive report.

None of the others had used the car much. I drove us to the hospital in the morning and back to the hotel at night. Unlike me, they'd stuck pretty close to the burn unit. But now they needed to get out; Janice or June needed something from a store, and Joanne decided she'd tag along, and then my mother decided she would too. I reluctantly gave up the car keys and said, "No, no, of course, here."

After they'd left, Al said, "There hasn't been any change."

I knew Al was doing what we all did—trying to let everybody else know the latest news on John's condition. But it bothered me that he happened to know John's condition just then, and that he knew the circumstances of the explosion, and that he knew what John's last days were like, and that he probably really knew John and I didn't.

As much as I hated it, I had to turn to Al for answers, and fast. With the rest of them gone, this might be one of my last chances to talk to John alone, and although I didn't know what I was going to say, I was pretty sure I wouldn't be able to say it in front of anybody else.

"So, was John happy?" I said.

"Happy?" Al said. "Oh yeah, he loved it in Bullhead City, on the river and everything. Or you mean the job?"

"Just in general," I said.

"Yeah, he was happy. He wasn't a partyer, like some of the guys, but he liked to get together and have dinner, you know, barbecues, that sort of thing. He didn't go for the casinos and that stuff, the shows."

"Did he have a lot of friends?"

"Well, John didn't have a *lot* of friends, but he had a few *good* friends. He was good people." Al caught himself and said, "Is. Is good people."

I let out a short, sad laugh. "He doesn't have much time left."

"I don't know," Al said. "He could still make it. We just have to put our faith in Jesus. Maybe it's God's will to take him, but God could save him too. If you have faith in—"

"What kind of car did he drive?" I said.

"What?" Al said.

"Car," I said. "His car. What kind was it?"

"You want to know what kind of car he drove?"

"Yeah," I said. Then I added, "It's sort of related to what you were saying."

Al nodded, seemingly trying to figure out the connection between life, death, God, and driving.

I was too.

Al said, "Well, let's see. He didn't really drive a car."

I leaned closer.

"It was a truck," Al said.

"A truck," I said.

"A pickup," Al said.

"Of course!" I said, as if solving a great riddle of the ages. It made perfect sense that my brother would drive a pickup, something he could take off road in the desert; after all, he lived there. I imagined the sort of fire-breathing rig my brother would drive, and how you'd probably need a ladder to step up into it. "Ford, right?" I said.

Al thought about it for a moment. "I don't think so," he said.

"Three-quarter ton?" I said.

"It was just a little pickup."

"Half-ton," I said. "Probably better in the sand. Four-wheel drive, right?"

"Uh, I don't think so," he said.

"But it had a big engine, didn't it? Did it have glass-pack exhausts?"

"I doubt it," Al said. "It was just a little stock pickup. You know, a fleet model."

"A sleeper!" I said. "I'll bet it hauled ass. Was it a Chevy? A Dodge?"

"Look," he said, "it was just a little stock Toyota pickup."

I slumped back on the stiff couch as if wounded. "Oh, Jesus!"

"What is it?" Al said.

"A Toyota," I said.

The thought of my brother driving a stock little Toyota pickup saddened me beyond all proportion. I wandered over to the ER to cheer myself up, and to figure out what I was going to tell him.

When I walked back, Al Laven was hunched forward, thinking. I sat down beside him and did a bit of thinking myself.

"The truck was very plain," Al said.

"What?" I said.

"The pickup, John's pickup. But it got good gas mileage. I remember him saying that."

I tried to wave away what Al was saying. He simply couldn't understand what I was getting at, and I realized that I didn't either.

"Even when he towed his Jet Skis, it got good mileage."

"His what?" I said.

"His Jet Skis," Al said. "That's what he got the truck for."

"He had Jet Skis?" I said, sitting up.

"Oh yeah, he was great on them, nobody better on the river."

"Jet Skis. Jet Skis."

"Yeah," Al said. "You sort of ride them like a—"

"Like a motorcycle," I said.

"On the water," he said.

I was smiling and weeping at the thought of my brother hauling ass through the desert on the Colorado River on the boating equivalent of a motorcycle. That seemed perfect.

I stood up and Al said, "Are you okay?"

"I'm fine," I said, and put my hand on his shoulder. "I'll be back in a while. I've got to tell my brother something."

I stood beside my brother's hospital bed and watched the nurse check the latest array of machines. John's seizure the day before, the doctor told me, was a sign that the end was near. Looking at my little notepad, opening my mouth to speak, I realized that whatever words came out, I wanted John to hear, or not, in private. I asked the nurse if she'd mind giving us a few minutes alone, and she smiled and suddenly was gone.

John's skin was still swollen, but its once-bright-red color had changed almost completely to dead yellow. You could see where catheters had been jabbed into his groin, his arms; where his skin had been debrided and wrapped with gauze. Standing there, you could read the heroic efforts the doctors had made to save his life. His body was like a battlefield.

A machine pushed each breath in and pulled each breath out. He was heavily drugged, and as his systems shut down, who could know for sure if his hearing was the first or last to go? But it seemed important, telling him. I was still angry that he hadn't spoken to me for five years, and angry that he'd probably had good reason, and angry that I'd gone along with it, and angry that we hadn't reconciled, and angry that he would die just as my life was beginning to take shape. But along with the anger was a very real grief—for all the same reasons. The two went together perfectly, grief and anger; sometimes it was hard to tell them apart, and sometimes they were identical.

I must have been alone with John in the burn unit before, but now we were alone for a purpose, a reckoning, a good-bye. I felt embarrassed and weak, yet resolved; my throat was swollen, my lips trembled, and my eyes burned with uncried tears.

I speak of John as if he was an actual presence in this teary good-bye, but his body was ravaged and motionless except for the machine-aided breaths that were pumped into his lungs. There wasn't much of him still working. But his presence of a lifetime was there. I felt it, and knew I'd have to speak honestly to it, just as that presence had always spoken to me. And still speaks to me.

But it is the small truths, the small kindnesses, that inform my memories of my brother. It was John who told me that when you're reeling in a spinning lure, a slightly erratic movement gets the fish excited. It was John who told me what "erratic" meant.

Still, it had been a long time since I'd really known my brother—longer even than the five years since he'd spoken to me. There was much that I just didn't know about him. I didn't know what he went through in the Marine Corps's basic training or on that flight to

Vietnam. I didn't know the loneliness that followed his divorce—didn't even know why he'd married her in the first place. I didn't know if he'd been happy at that job. I didn't know his secret dreams, what he really wanted from life. I didn't know why, exactly, he stopped talking to me, and didn't know if he'd ever planned on speaking to me again, and didn't know if he regretted those years of silence between us.

I did know a few things about my brother. I knew that he loved the desert, and that here he found solitude and beauty and a place to drive fast. He liked to drive fast. He liked fast cars not just because they were fast but also because they were well made. He liked to make things right, to work with his hands until he'd made something perfect, for example, a perfectly tuned engine. He loved that sound and the feeling that went with it: being pressed back against the seat as the engine unwound and the car surged forward through the desert. He liked driving cars and he also liked riding motorcycles, which offered another level of freedom: the ability to go off road in any direction, and to go fast over rough terrain as a way of proving himself and of making a difficult ride into a thing of beauty.

I knew that my brother would want to live in the desert and have a house not far from the Colorado River. I knew that he'd even work at a place like Southern California Edison if it allowed him to live here. I knew he wouldn't mind driving a shitty little truck if he could use it to tow something important, in this case Jet Skis, which could haul ass up and down the Colorado River with him standing there as if on a motorcycle, the hot wind against his face, the cold water splashing up.

It occurred to me that I wasn't mad at my brother

anymore, and I knew that in the end, when it mattered, he wasn't mad at me. And I knew that I loved him very much, and that he loved me. And in this there was considerable grace.

On the longest day of the year, I told my brother he was going to die. I don't imagine he heard me and I don't even remember what I said—but I do remember a kind of clearing. I stopped crying and leaned close to him, and I said softly, clearly, "Hey, buddy. . ."

On the day of John's funeral, Los Angeles felt nearly as hot as Phoenix, as if the heat of the desert had come home with us, and the desert is not a place to wear a jacket and tie.

I was wearing a jacket and tie. I'd gone out to a big mall and actually shopped for something to wear, knowing that in this heat I wouldn't want to wear that stuff for one minute longer than I had to, and that I'd probably never want to wear it again.

This had been complicated somewhat because I also wanted to look like a writer. I *was* a writer now, or would be any minute. The *Mississippi Review* number 39 had been delayed. I'd called the managing editor as soon as I got back to Los Angeles, and she told me that the issue had just arrived—she was holding it in her hand. She said she'd send my contributor's copies right away.

So for those few days before the funeral I thought about the end of my brother's life and the beginning of mine. The two seemed linked, and I hated this notion, partly because it trivialized John, as if any *thing*—a mag-azine, a book—could equal a life. But I also hated that notion because I knew it would never go away and that there was probably a reason for it: that one of the proud-est moments in my life was accompanied by the very saddest.

Nonetheless, I stalked through the mall and won-dered, as I grieved for my brother, what to wear.

Anything woolen was out, of course. I looked at silk jackets, but they were too expensive and too hot, and none of the linen jackets I found was black. I must have made three trips around the mall, hunting even in the stores whose window mannequins looked like 1950s space aliens. Finally I just gave up. I went into—I don't know—Sears, J. C. Penney, and bought a dark, light-weight jacket that looked like something a new detective might wear to the scene of a murder.

Which was, I realize now, appropriate.

Before the funeral, we sat in our mother's little living room in much the same way that we'd sat in the waiting room, all of us with nothing much to say—or so much to say that we were dumbstruck.

I thought about how we'd all grown up here, all five of us, in this three-bedroom house, and how the house had stayed the same but seemed different. When I was little, the house was large and in places mysterious: my father's dresser, my sisters' closets. When I was older, after I'd moved away, the house seemed cramped; it was filled with my father and his years of illness, and when he died, just ten months ago, the house didn't exactly seem bigger, but it somehow had more light.

We had the windows and the front door open to let in a breeze. There was no breeze. It was just still and hot and we'd soon have to go in our stiff clothes to John's funeral; he'd died, he really was dead, and the funeral would be the proof.

This was in some sense a relief, just as it had been a relief when he'd finally died and we scrambled out of Phoenix. But it wasn't a relief to have to go back to Rose Hills, where my father and one grandmother and one uncle were buried. I knew Rose Hills a little too well.

The limousine came right on time, but I'd decided to drive to the funeral by myself, although my cousin Tim showed up and went with me. So we all walked out of the house together, just as the mailman arrived.

"Oh, good, you're here," he said.

We all stopped and stared at him.

"I've got a package for you. I'll be right back."

He was gone before any of us could say anything, but I knew what the package was.

"I'll wait for him," I said. "I'll catch up." My mother and sisters got into the limousine and drove away, and I waited for the mailman, who took longer than he said he would. I was sweating in my new jacket and wishing that I'd gone on; the mailman could deliver it the next day. I was about ready to leave anyway when he came up with the package. The typewritten label was addressed to me, and the return address read MISSISSIPPI REVIEW.

I raced to Rose Hills, only a few miles away. When I was a kid, the constant funeral processions often screwed up my bicycle riding. I drove through the gate and soon figured out that I'd driven through the wrong gate. Then I drove to the wrong chapel. Finally I had to ask for directions from a gardener who didn't speak English. I evidently didn't know Rose Hills as well as I thought.

Everybody was already seated when Tim and I hurried in. He went and sat in the main chapel, and I went and sat in a little booth for the immediate family—the same booth I'd sat in ten months earlier, with John, at our father's funeral.

I don't remember much of what happened at John's funeral, except that I didn't take off my mirrored Vuarnet sunglasses, didn't cry much, and that when it was over, I drove away from there as fast as I could.

But I remember the closed casket in the front of the chapel. Somebody had enlarged a photograph of John and surrounded it with flowers. As everybody gazed teary-eyed and grieving and exhausted at the photograph, there was John staring back at us, smiling.

I finished the first draft of this book on the day I started becoming older than my brother. I never imagined that such a thing might be possible—the little brother older than the big one—and in some ways I still don't.

But when I look at photographs of my brother, my sisters, my parents, I'm still amazed at the transformation of a life. I stare at my favorite, the one of my father holding my brother, and can't help but smile. The photograph is black and white, and my father, probably just off work, is wearing a gabardine shirt and slacks that look like a smart military uniform. My father's smiling proudly and holding one hand high in the air, the way a waiter might carry a tray. John, at two or three, is standing in the palm of his hand. His arms are angled outward for balance, and his expression is one of bewilderment—at this incredible height and strength, this incredible moment, a life held firmly in a hand.

I think about my brother when I drive, and I drive a lot. I am a driver. I drive to relax, and to think, and to feel the pleasure of setting out on the road and living between two worlds: where I'm going and where I've been. Driving always renews my faith in destinations.

When I drive, I'm also with my brother. Sometimes I'll head out into the desert, on the same freeway that John took on his last trip, when his body was driven from Phoenix to Los Angeles. Part of this freeway replaced the old Route 66, which was decommissioned the same year John died. I like to think that I'm driving fast, although my old Ford pickup doesn't go fast. But no matter—there I go in my imaginary fast car, and sometimes I see my brother driving, and sometimes I see myself riding shotgun, feel myself pressed back against the seat as he floors the gas pedal, and suddenly we are very clear and the rest of the world is a blur.

Sometimes I'll pull over to stretch. I love the dry desert air, the alkaline hills, the smell of sage and creosote. Once, I pulled over at a place that looked familiar; I saw a dirt road and drove down it, then saw the floodplain and the foothills where John and Mickey Otten and I had gone target shooting a few days before John's induction into the Marine Corps. I walked across the sand, across the many dry creeks, and remembered John giving me the Remington rifle that Christmas.

And I remembered something I'd forgotten. It was raining that day, a light, steady rain, and the runoff cut fast-moving streams in the sandy mud. As we were hiking back to the Corvette, it started raining harder, and we had to jump the rising streams.

When we came to a wider stream, maybe six or eight feet across, John looked at Mickey. I just stood there between them. I didn't hear either of them say any-thing—with all the water running it was hard to hear. It seems now that I often didn't hear what my brother had to say.

But on that rainy day thirty years ago, John slogged across the swift-moving stream and, when he got to the other side, turned toward us and smiled. Then he said, very clearly, "Okay." Mickey lifted my rifle by its strap and slung it across his shoulder. Then he picked me up and tossed me across the stream and into my brother's arms.

A NOTE ON THE TYPE

This book was set in Fairfield, the first typeface from the hand of the distinguished American artist and engraver Rudolph Ruzicka (1883–1978). In its structure Fairfield displays the sober and sane qualities of the master craftsman whose talent has long been dedicated to clarity. It is this trait that accounts for the trim grace and vigor, the spirited design and sensitive balance, of this original typeface.

Rudolph Ruzicka was born in Bohemia and came to America in 1884. He set up his own shop, devoted to wood engraving and printing, in New York in 1913 after a varied career working as a wood engraver, in photoengraving and banknote printing plants, and as an art director and freelance artist. He designed and illustrated many books, and was the creator of a considerable list of individual prints—wood engravings, line engravings on copper, and aquatints.

Composed by Stratford Publishing Services,
Brattleboro, Vermont
Printed and bound by Quebecor Printing,
Martinsburg, West Virginia
Designed by Virginia Tan

AAW - 6891